SOUTHERN
CROSS

PAUL CLARK

SOUTHERN CROSS

*Lost and Found
on the Streets
and in the Jungles of
Peru*

BPS Books
Toronto, Canada
www.bpsbooks.net
A division of Bastian Publishing Services Ltd.

Distributed by
Ingram Book Group

Cataloguing in Publication Data available
from Library and Archives Canada.

Editorial: Donald G. Bastian, Bastian Publishing Services Ltd.,
www.bastianpubserv.com
Cover photo design by Michaela Miron, with images
from istock, shutterstock, and the author.
Interior Text Design: Tannice Goddard, Soul Oasis Networking

To Marty,
my wife and closest friend

CONTENTS

PREFACE

"*P*aul, have you ever written up any of these stories?" Then, "When you do, I'll be the first to order a copy."

I heard this so often from people who had come to Peru to serve with us on work or medical teams that I finally decided — "someday" — to do something. *Mañana* is our word for it.

However, it was not so much the constant prompting from all sides as my own inner urge to tell a story that needed telling that made me sit down and actually start writing. I knew that people must hear of the countless children who live in constant fear: the throwaway kids of our modern consumer society and little ones who cry at night in their hiding places, hearing only the echo of their own voices.

With this book now finally completed, I want to express my gratitude first of all to my wife, Marty, who shares my passion to reach out with Christ's love to those who suffer. Without her diligent help, this book would never have been written.

Claude Simmonds was a faithful friend and mentor for many years when the path was steep and rocky. My gratitude to Betty, his widow, who, along with Scripture Union Canada, provided the means to get this manuscript into the hands of the printer.

Most endeavors are backed by well-wishers, and I have had my share of them, but it was John Irwin who decided to make this one happen, when he read the manuscript while on a tour down the Rhine River with his wife, Eleanor. And so he has.

May you, Don Bastian, my ever-so-patient editor, and others who have had a part in this project, share in the lasting results of making known to the world the plight of the poor and the grace and greatness of God in responding to their deepest need.

INTRODUCTION

I well remember, back in the 1940s when I was a child, my father sitting at the foot of my bed and telling me bedtime stories. They were all true and about real people. I loved them all. I now think that he wanted me to enjoy the Bible stories most, but except for Samson and Delilah and David and Goliath, the ones that really captured me were those about his experiences in the early 1920s among the Yavaré of Brazil, the headhunting Jívaro of Peru, and his favorite tribe, the Ashaninka. I never wearied of hearing them. Daddy was my hero and I always wanted to be like him. I so badly wanted to grow up. I wanted to meet a real *Shambari* (Ashaninka chief), to see an anaconda chase a canoe, to see a shrunken head. But it was to be a few years yet before I would really know my dad — before I'd understand what truly made him the man I loved, and what gave him such passion and single-mindedness.

When that day came, I was sixteen. It was the day I asked God to take my life — hook, line, and sinker — and use me in whatever manner he wished.

About the time I graduated from Wheaton College, I made a list of seven characteristics of the perfect wife for me. I'd wait as long as necessary, but I would never marry till I found her. My friends, one by one, married. By the time I reached the age of twenty-eight, things were looking a bit grim. I was fully aware that my demands were possibly excessive, but after this long a wait, I wasn't about to give up on them.

Then it was that I met and married Martha (Marty) Jane Spilman. Therein lies a long story, and I wish I could tell it here. Suffice it to say that we have worked with Scripture Union, one way or another, for forty-five years: as volunteers while we were both school teachers, and then, from 1969 until the present, on the staff. Over all of those years, we have seen some pretty amazing things happen.

One of the first things we did was to head into Amazonia and set up what was to become a bright light for the gospel in a very dark Peruvian jungle. We called it Nokimoshiritaiki, or Kimo for short. This was to be a place where boys and girls from deep within the tropical forest, from the high Andean mountains, and from the distant cities, would encounter God through his Word and be able to say, "I (no) joyful (kimo) in my spirit (shiri) am (taiki)!"

Kimo was a wonderful place. That's where our little Janie developed her fascination with snakes and where Billy gained the experience that now holds him in good stead leading visiting work teams into the jungle. But it was Johnny, our youngest, who would become my Jungle Jim. I still call him Quiriquincho (Ashaninka for armadillo) and have a picture of him riding a tree trunk down the fast-flowing and dangerous Chanchamayo River.

Then Kimo was destroyed by the Shining Path terrorists, and it would take years for us to rebuild it. During those years, an ever-growing number of boys were condemned to live their lives in abandonment. Many of them eventually came to Kimo.

Just a few years ago, I was made an Honorary Chief of the Ashaninka tribe. I sat in the middle of the circle. Around me were many Indians in full regalia, *achiote* etchings on their faces. While they chanted and placed the feathered *corona* on my head, my thoughts raced back to the good old days of bedtime stories. My daddy would have been so proud.

This book is a selection of stories describing the lives that we've seen transformed by God. The settings of these stories span the jungles, plateaus, mountains, and cities of this wild and remote country of Peru. The incidents described may seem far-off and shocking. And yet each life was touched by the same one and loving God.

I

CALIXTO
"I'll Tell Him the Next Time"

*I*t was a dark night in the Peruvian jungle. The stars looked like so many diamonds scattered across a background of velvet.

"Maniro," said Notomi to his eldest son, "you are the last one to take your place at my fire, and you ought to have been the first."

Notomi was chief, and it was no secret that he wanted his son to follow in his footsteps. But Maniro would have to prove himself as a fearless warrior and a leader of men. This would not be easy because the law of the jungle is implacable, making no allowances for weakness or mistakes.

Maniro was tempted to point to the wild boar that he had just dragged into the clearing and whose blood still smudged his hands and *cushma* (rough cotton gown), but on second thought he decided to limit himself to a polite, "Yes, Father."

The dancing flames intermittently revealed the painted faces of the forest dwellers, whose bodies in turn threw shadows on the thatch of the primitively built huts behind them. It was good to be huddled together around the safety of the fire and under the ever-watchful eye of Notomi.

When the sun sets, the god of the Ashaninka Indians is gone, and although this is a daily occurrence, it is nonetheless frightening. At night the jungle comes to life. Although the dreaded boa sleeps, other forms of serpents, vampire bats, and the feared *otorongo* (jaguar) set out under the cover of darkness in search of food and water. But these can be dealt with. For centuries the men of the great forests of the Amazon have perfected ways to protect themselves from prowlers of the night. The real fear that grips the heart of every man, woman, and child is the ever-present thought of Kamari, the evil spirits. Their passion is to hurt, harm, and kill. They constantly seek revenge.

For the Ashaninkas, Kamari were at one time human themselves. Demons live underground and make raids into Ashaninka territory, lurking in the forests and teeming in the waters. They prompt the most horrendous fears, fears that grip the soul of every Indian.

The gentle breeze caused by the passing of demons, known as Atantsi Kamari, causes sickness. Should one so much as catch a glimpse of a demon itself, instant death is the result. The Monkoite demons forage at night in search of the souls of children, while the Tsomi-kirino search for older people, collect them in their stomachs, and transform them into the dreaded Viracocha, white men, for whom Notomi harbored particularly intense hatred.

The men who sat around the crackling campfire that night wore their red paint lavishly, but the women applied it with taste, expressing their mood in the designs they chose to draw in thin, often intricate lines. An arrow on the cheek, for example, indicated happiness and the disposition to engage in friendly banter with the men, whereas a scorpion, thinly etched in black, was fair warning of a foul mood.

"Tell us a story, Notomi," said one of the younger children with a quick smile that contrasted sharply with the sullen mood of the older folk.

"Quickly," said Notomi's youngest son. "Kashiri will soon appear over the trees and we will have to sleep. Tell us about the Viracocha."

This was one of many stories that were often told around the fire. Neither children nor adults ever grew weary of hearing them. In the absence of writing, it is the collection of stories handed down from generation to generation that explains to the Ashaninka the meaning of life and helps them understand what they see around them.

The fire now was low and just the right size, and there was barely a curling wisp of smoke rising toward the sky. Notomi leaned forward and with a quick glance toward his eldest son began to speak. "Yes, I will tell the story of Viracocha, whom we have fortunately never seen, and who lives very far away. Someday perhaps Maniro will be the one to tell you this same story.

"First, I'll tell you about Pava and about Kashiri. Pava likes me to talk about him. That is why even our dances are for him. Every morning, just as the *chicharras* stop their screeching and the *coro-coro* begin to fly, Pava rises above the tallest trees and brightens up the sky. All day he keeps us warm. In the evening he becomes very beautiful before leaving us on his way to Irimaka (the world of evil spirits) and darkness. While he is there, Kashiri takes over.

"Pava was born a normal person just like us, but he became hotter and hotter and would have soon burned up all the jungle. Finally a bird, Kentimpard, wrapped him in many *cushmas* and carried him into the sky. So I have been told.

"As for Kashiri, the bright one of the night, he, too, was a man. But this was long ago, when men ate earth and termites. He killed his wife and started running. When his relatives were about to catch up to him, he rose into the sky where he now keeps killing people and eating them. He now gets thin when he remembers how much he had to run to escape his angry family. He then starts fattening up by eating the souls of people he kills.

"The only one worse than Kashiri is Viracocha. He lives at River's End. Only our ancestors once saw him. His skin is white like Kashiri's. Pava has never kept him warm and browned his skin. Like the otorongo and the howler monkey, he has hair on his face. We see Kashiri, but have never seen Viracocha. This is how the story was told to me."

For the next couple of hours the chief related this and other stories, as one, and then another, fell asleep or wandered off to their huts. He ended with the usual, "This is how the story was told to me" and quietly made his way to the safety of his own hut.

⸺

As Notomi lay there, little could he imagine that on a sandbank just a few bends downstream, a Viracocha sat beside a similar campfire, looking forward to the rising of Kashiri.

This white man was anxiously awaiting his encounter with the legendary chief Notomi, absolute ruler of the Anacayali River and its Ashaninka inhabitants.

His general knowledge of the jungle, the rumors he had heard on the larger Pachitea River of the particular viciousness of Notomi, and his common sense told him that he was headed for disaster. Had not the arrows of the Anacayali Ashaninkas just killed a Franciscan monk before he even reached the mouth of the river? Had not this particular branch of the tribe sufficiently established its hatred of the Viracocha? Surely there must be some good reason for his being the first Viracocha to venture this far upstream.

And there was. It was not based on logic or history or good common sense. It was based on trust. Trust in God, the one who held absolute power over all the forces of the jungle darkness.

It had been a long day. Their day of travel had started at early dawn. Tushi and Kiriko, two young Indians from the Pachitea who had come to help the white man on his journey, had done a good job of poling the dugout canoe up the ever-narrowing river. The three men had seen small animals darting in and out of the jungle and heard monkeys and birds chattering and chirping in the branches that hung low over the riverbanks. But they saw no sign of what they were looking for until late that afternoon: a small cut piece of balsa wood — which had obviously formed part of a raft — floating slowly downstream, gave them absolute assurance that the headwaters of the Anacayali were still inhabited.

The sandbank was long and narrow, and the fire they built there was equidistant between river and jungle. This would offer maximum protection during the night hours. The meal — turtle eggs dug out of the sand, and fresh monkey meat roasted over the fire — was good.

Noticing that he seemed miles away, Kiriko said, "Viracocha, you are not listening to our stories. Your soul is wandering into the forest."

"No, you have nothing to fear," the white man replied. "My soul will not leave my body tonight. It will stay here while I sleep. Then tomorrow we shall continue our journey to the place the balsa log came from. Perhaps then we shall meet Notomi."

This seemed to put the men at ease. They continued poking away at the fire while their companion moved just a slight distance away and lay down for the night.

The Viracocha was none other than my own dad, Raymond Brooke Clark. He came to Peru in 1922 from Jamaica via Brazil. His search for a tribe to evangelize started at the mouth of the Amazon and ended in Ashaninka territory under the auspices of the Christian and Missionary Alliance. In later years, when I was still young, he and I often talked about the stars. He had impressed on me the greatness of God. And when it came to the night sky, he had a particular spot in his heart for the Southern Cross.

On that night, many years ago now, on the banks of the Anacayali River, Dad was in all likelihood watching the sky as the fiery cross rose above the giant trees and matted undergrowth on the far side of the stream. Two lines form every cross, and at one point they intersect. So it was to be with the lives of Dad and Notomi, who for many years had followed very different courses, yet were one day to cross paths. The eternal destiny of one would hinge on the faithfulness of the other.

The fire burned slowly through the night. Tushi and Kiriki slept fitfully, while Dad happily committed his life and the events of the coming day into the hands of him "who never sleepeth."

Tushi and Kiriki greeted the rising sun with a wild display of enthusiastic shrieks and screams. This was their way of saluting the one who brought warmth and light and happiness into their lives. For them, this moment marked the beginning of a new day. More than that, it put an end to yet another dreaded night.

All nights are feared by the Ashaninkas. Next to death itself, they are most afraid of night. They have healthy respect for the large leopard-like cat, the otorongo, but it can be handled. After all, while the Ashaninkas are not be as strong as it and other wildlife, they are decidedly very clever. As for the dreaded Viracocha, there is even a good chance of getting the better of him. But as for death, this is the one enemy that can never be conquered. The Indians hate the dark, for darkness is a foretaste of death itself.

More turtle eggs for breakfast, and they were back to another long day of tedious poling up the river. After many hours it was time to leave the water and follow the trail to the Ashaninka habitation.

"You will follow me, Viracocha," said Kiriki. "You must not talk. Your voice is not good to upriver people."

Kiriki added: "Chief Notomi and his men will soon know that two Ashaninkas are leading a Viracocha to his place. He has eyes in every tree. He will summon his men and instruct them. When we get to the clearing, there will be no one there. That is the way of the Ashaninka."

They walked on at an ever-faster pace. It came as a relief to break out of the steaming, insect-infested bush right into the jungle clearing. This was the heart of the Anakiali River Kingdom.

As expected, the clearing was abandoned, but showed every indication that it had been hurriedly vacated only minutes before. A large, sizzling *huanganga* (wild boar) was roasting over the log fire. Tree trunks hollowed out to make large basins were brimming with bubbling *masato* (fermented yuca manioc drink).

"Listen carefully, Viracocha," advised Tushi, in a voice more hushed and deliberate than usual. "The men are not far from here. They may well be positioned so as to be observing us right now."

Tushi continued: "When they reach the center of the clearing, they will stop and all turn facing us or giving us their backs. If they face us, they are greeting us with a welcome. All will be well. If they turn their backs on us, however ..." He stopped short.

Without the slightest sound, with no appreciable movement of leaf or snapping of twig, five Ashaninka warriors made their formal appearance. First in line was a tall and austere-looking Indian armed with a bow and a bundle of exceptionally large arrows. As he drew near, it became obvious that he was an older man, yet he showed no signs of weakness. He was followed by a man very much in his prime: broad shouldered, unusually strong, and possessing a determination and arrogance that made it easy to identify him. "He had a very strong face and the bull neck of a Caesar," Dad told me later. This was, without doubt, Notomi.

This man was followed by two young men, and then by one whose face clearly denoted anger and hate through a thick coating of red *achiote*. All of them had quickly spread this on their faces for the occasion.

With no fanfare whatsoever, the five Ashaninkas came to a halt opposite their visitors. At a simple, one-word command from the second man, they all turned sharply on their heels facing away from the Viracocha and his guides.

Kiriki was well on his way like a well-trained sprinter, and Tushi gave Dad a tug on the elbow in the direction of the nearest exit. The getaway would have to be fast. Fortunately, paddling would be quick downstream, and the poles could be disregarded. But a meandering river makes progress slow. Indians on foot can use the many trails and shortcuts through the forest to cut travelers off at one of the lower loops in the river.

And that is precisely what happened. Around the next bend, atop large outcrops of granite on both sides of the river, stood the Ashaninkas, armed with bows and slender *cana brava* arrows.

Dad told me years later that he panicked. Suddenly, in his heart, rest turned to anxiety, trust turned to fear, and doubt battled faith. God's promises seemed empty, his presence distant. A lifetime of dreams and countless prayers was now on the verge of extinction. All this and more crowded into his mind in a matter of seconds.

Then, just as a ray of light can break through the storm cloud, a sense of peace flooded my father's heart. It was incredible, he said: one of those moments in the life of a Christian one rarely talks about and then never lightly. One of those few times when you sense you are treading on holy ground.

My father and his two guides glided silently in their dugout canoe through the narrow passage below the stalwart Ashaninka warriors on either side with arrows poised.

Dad glanced back at the warriors. Something amazing was happening. As though paralyzed, the warriors could not fire. He glanced back again, and there they still stood.

Tushi and Kiriki had no explanation for it. It was later discovered that Notomi, the legendary Ashaninka chief, didn't either.

"Wait on the Big River," Tushi told my father.

"And never go up the Anacayali again," warned Kiriki. "Notomi will now want to meet you. He will want to know who protects you. If he comes to you, he will not harm you. Wait for him on the Big River."

Dad waited and waited. He and the men built two large thatched huts. And they waited more. Several moons passed. Dad learned that God is never in a hurry, and when Notomi — with some twenty of his warriors and their families — appeared, he learned also that God never arrives late.

Many more huts were built over the coming months as the families settled. At night they gathered around the campfire and listened. Notomi repeated his ancient stories, and Dad told his stories about Jesus and the Kingdom of God that awaits all who believe in him after they leave this world. He prayed that God through his Holy Spirit would break into the lives of these people he was growing to love and save them from the awful death of the Ashaninka warrior.

A year passed. And then, one day, the great Chief Notomi came down with "the fever," as malignant malaria was known. Notomi knew he would not recover.

The Ashaninka always want to die in the place of their birth, so Notomi ordered his men to take him up the Anacayali to his childhood home.

Some twenty canoes were readied and filled. The fleet set out at dawn to carry the great chief to his final resting place. Dad did not know whether any of them would ever come back.

The Ashaninka death scene is one of fear and terror, with the dying one grasping for one more breath before being carried away into the unknown underworld with its myriad of evil spirits awaiting yet another disembodied soul.

The next afternoon, Dad was surprised to see the twenty canoes coming back. He went down to the river's edge. The young man in the leading canoe got out.

"Chief Notomi died on the sandbank last night," he said. "We were all surprised that he left us so quietly. We had never seen that before. His last words to me were, 'Go back to the Big River tomorrow and tell Viracocha that I died and went to the place he told me about.'"

⁓

Like my father, I had two companions on my first trip into the jungle, in 1969. Ernesto Zavala and Leslie Hemery were teenagers who had come to faith in Jesus through the ministry of Scripture Union in Lima and were now ready to reach out to others.

After a long trek by bus over the 16,000-foot pass through the Andes, the three of us were greeted by our guide, Manuel, on the Chanchamayo River in Ashaninka territory.

We soon found ourselves on a steep trail. Ferns of every size and hue and trees from which vines hung close overhead, vying with one another to catch a glimpse of the tropical sun, held our attention the entire way up. Here was beauty at its most lavish, with vegetation of every exotic kind, so dense as to make passage difficult.

There had been a torrential rain the night before. We took turns slipping and falling into the sea of sticky clay. But we were so exhilarated that we didn't care. It was one of those fairy-tale mornings when birds dip low to touch the magic of the good earth and large, blue-winged butterflies try to reach just a little bit higher than usual to get a fleeting look at the full-blown blossoms in the tops of the jacaranda trees. It was now getting hotter and vapor could be seen missing in a thin, endless sheet through the tropical rainforest to form big puffy white clouds.

We stopped briefly from time to time, usually to drink from one of the streams we came across on our way up, sometimes just to catch our breath.

"Tired?" Manuel would inquire every once in a while.

"No, not at all," the three of us would lie in unison. "We do this every day. It's a breeze."

Manuel was fun, and although he kept up a wicked pace, we were glad he was along. Were he to have disappeared into thin air, we would probably still be trying to find our way out.

Suddenly we broke into the open onto a beautiful high plateau. The breeze, the sounds, the views were all incredible. In the distance I could see the wooded ridge that separated us from the valley of the Anacayali River. It was by now late afternoon and the jungle had broken into sound. The chicharra, crickets, and frogs vied with one another and with countless other insects and large beetles to announce yet another night.

"This is it," said Manuel.

"¡Qué más!" (What more could we want?) said Ernesto.

They were both right. This was the place where Kimo would be built. It was far more than we deserved, a prayer answered beyond our dreams or expectations.

That was our first trip to Kimo; there would be many more to follow.

On my second trip I was introduced to Calixto. In his early twenties, tall for a Peruvian and thin, he was shy but friendly. He was not an accomplished carpenter and never claimed to be one. But he was willing to build something rustic, which was exactly what we wanted.

Calixto would change my life. I knew that he was the first person in Kimo who was going to hear the gospel from me. Why wait for the first campers from the coast or children from Ashaninka land? Calixto, too, needed to know that Jesus had died to set him free and risen to await him in heaven some day. But I had never found it easy to talk to anyone about their eternal destiny despite the fact that I so very much wanted them to become followers of my Lord.

"Someone else will probably do it," was my usual excuse, but that couldn't possibly apply to Calixto. "Like who?" I answered myself. "Exactly who else is going to come up this trail, onto the top of this hill in the middle of this remote jungle, to tell Calixto that Jesus loves him?"

So I told God that I would ... next time.

"Calixto ¿qué tienes?" (Calixto, what's wrong?) I inquired when I looked up and saw him seated on the pile of rough lumber with his hammer in his hand.

"No sé" (I don't know), he said. "I don't feel too well. My face is hot. Do you mind if I go down to La Merced to buy some medicine?"

"Of course not," I said, and gave him ten *soles*. "What's more, I'll come with you."

We parted company in the town. It was a Tuesday afternoon. "I'll be back on Friday," I said, and headed for the bus company and my long trip back over the high Andes to the coast.

On Friday I was back. This time I knew my way and made it through the jungle alone. When I arrived at Kimo, Manuel was at the top leaning against a *palo rosa* tree next to the heaped-up lumber.

"Hola, Manuel," I said. "Where is Calixto?"

Manuel hesitated, then looked at the ground, then looked at me. "Calixto is dead." He looked back at the ground.

I grappled for words, but none came. I sat down on a rough plank. Just how many thoughts can pass through a man's dizzy mind in a split second? Thoughts that all put together add up to nothing, yet leave pain. Pain that in my case all too quickly transformed itself into an immense sensation of guilt.

Manuel broke the silence. "Calixto died yesterday of yellow fever. He was buried this morning."

"Oh God," I began to cry. "Oh God, Calixto is gone. I was the one who was to have told him about you. Remember I said I would, next time? But there was no next time. You gave me just one chance, and I missed it. Oh God, I beg you, forgive me!"

I struggled with my guilt far more than I wish to remember, but one thing it taught me: I needed to talk to Manuel, and in the coming weeks I did.

I remembered how my dad had struggled yet found his faith just when he needed it the most. Construction of Kimo could not stop because of my inner struggle and my inability to accept God's forgiveness.

It was not easy to find someone to finish the big hut, especially the roof, because the Ashaninka only cut the humiro palm for the thatch at full moon. They say when Kashiri's belly is full, he is happy. He has filled it with the souls of the dead. That means he doesn't notice when you cut the forest. If you chop branches when he is thin and hungry, he will punish you by sending termites to eat your roof.

Manuel finished the job and over the following years became my very close friend. But I would never forget Calixto.

A tank was built for swimming, poles for hanging hammocks under the palm roofs were put in place, and we were set to go. At our first camp, three young teenagers came to faith in Christ, and then the enemy struck back. A boa constrictor joined us in the tank. Two of our boys were attacked by vampire bats. Fear threatened to paralyze us. However, the week ended on a high note and the kids left, happy.

The next camp was disrupted by an alarming number of tarantulas, and one of the older boys had to be taken home across the Andes because of a serious breach of conduct.

As the months and years went by, we would have much bigger problems than tarantulas. Kimo was never intended to be a place of confrontation, but looking back, I suppose we hadn't really done our homework: we had no idea of the incredible things that were going to happen. We were about to engage in hand-to-hand combat with darkness itself, and we were not that well prepared. We quickly learned that "we struggle not against flesh and blood, but against powers and principalities in high places" (Ephesians 6:12). With the battle lines clearly drawn, we made our beachhead on the sandbanks of the Chanchamayo River.

For Kimo's home, we had selected a beautiful place on the edge of the Ashaninka tribal territory. We had inadvertently awakened the giant, confronting the powerful Ashaninka deity right in the center of his power. He had held sway in this distant forest for far too long. He had his *Brujos* (witch doctors) strategically placed in every clearing, and firmly embedded in every mind his lies about Nonki, the Demon

Bat, and the Great Gateway to the Underworld. He was accepted as King of Demons and obeyed all across the region as Ruler of the Six Rivers.

As we would discover, Ashaninka was just the beginning. Fear, poverty, spiritism, abuse, and sheer terror marked the lives of many I would soon encounter in the deep jungles of Amazonia and the dark, foreboding alleys off busy Andean streets. Corruption, disease, drugs, politics, and violence were destroying the lives of millions here in this ancient country. The great lesson I was about to learn was that although circumstances and settings can be vastly different, God's dealing with all men and women, girls and boys, is the same. He meets us all at the point of our greatest need and, having heard our cry for help and sensing our anguish of soul, responds with compassion and love. I was to witness love at work in this ancient, troubled, and mysterious land of Peru.

2

ZICO
No Longer Alone

*E*ver since, at the age of seven, he had last seen his mother and had said goodbye to home, never to return, this wounded little boy carried far too great a burden.

Zico was born in 1985 in the mountain town of Tambo to a woman named Carmela. She already had two children and there were several more to come. Victim of the abuse of one man after another, she grew increasingly unhappy. In a place where women must depend on men for everything, Carmela secretly envied the woman next door who had four children, all by the same man.

"She's lucky," Carmela mused as she patted baby Zico and tickled him under the chin. "But she doesn't have you, my little boy. You are ever so much prettier than any of hers."

Her optimism became more and more forced. It soon became impossible for this thin little woman to face life. As years went by, she added more men and more children to her list. She had heard of the proverbial overloaded lifeboat and knew that in her case, too, one more and they would all sink.

Carmela's current man — as all the others had been, for that matter — was poor. He worked in a mine and spent most of his meager salary on drink. Very little money ever made it home. He always insisted that it was enough, that he loved Carmela but not all her children. "Only the baby is mine," he repeated a thousand times. "Only the baby, do you not understand? The others are yours. They are your problem, not mine!"

Zico bore the brunt of this man's frustration. Confident that punishment would drive the older ones away on their own, the man regularly beat the boy and withheld food from him. Carmela defended her son and for a while managed to sneak potatoes to him that she had hidden behind the coal stove. But soon that was discovered and the game was over. To save the others, Zico had to go. From now on his life was to be lived on the streets, or even worse, in abandoned mines.

To the north and high above Kimo are abandoned mines once used to extract copper, lead, and zinc, and that is where Zico lived.

Zico sat on the rounded edge of a big rock at the entrance to an abandoned tunnel that led deep into the earth. Every now and then the sun shone through the massive white clouds. It kept the rock warm, so he stretched out on it, his cheek touching the rough surface. It felt so good.

"If only it would stay this way," he thought, then quickly sat up. He could not afford to keep his eyes for very long off the dirt road just below that led to Tambo. That was the way policemen came into the mining camp, and Zico had had more than his share of encounters with them.

Now another cloud darkened the sky. Twin passions struggled within him: the passion to love and the passion to hate. Try as he may, there seemed no one left in his life to love. His mind raced toward his mother, but he blocked the thought. It was too painful. It was much easier to hate, but that chewed away at the real little Zico, the one who had gurgled when his mother patted his little back and who later ran errands for her as he grew to be a loving son.

There wasn't much to be gained by brooding, but he found it hard not to. His attention was diverted — just as well — when a condor flew by. Viewed by people around Kimo as possessing an evil spirit, the condor is the king of birds, strong and beautiful, but above all, free. Zico wondered what the bird thought when it looked down on him on the big, warm rock.

This day was unusual, for Zico rarely ventured out in the daytime. He started back down the tunnel. His home was deep in the earth. The only way down was through long, narrow shafts. It was awful, but it was the only place near Tambo where an abandoned kid could feel safe from the police. So this is where he lived with two other small boys whose fate had been the same as his.

It was bitterly cold at the end of the tunnel, but there was a slightly wider part where the boys could lie down, overlapping one another like puppy dogs. Except for the occasional visit to the rock, they only left the tunnel when they could bear their hunger no longer. And the only really safe time to do so was at dusk or at night.

The best time to steal was in the early evening. They would go together and snatch a bag, or every now and then a purse. They would then sell or exchange their goods in the streets of Tambo and head off toward the market area, where they were known by a group of street vendors.

Sometimes they exchanged the stolen goods right there for a bowl of soup or a plate of rice and *mote* (boiled Andean corn). It was the high point of their existence. And they always kept the last bit to trade at the corner of Junin and Casma for an ounce of *terokal*, the glue they drugged themselves with once they were back deep inside the mine. This routine was only broken by visits to the *comisaría* (police station) when they were caught. The police would give them a sound thrashing and put them back out into the blinding cold street.

This life went on, day in and day out, for months and months — in fact, for over two years — before Zico finally gave up.

It was late one night when he decided to go up and sit on the rock. The stars were incredibly bright as stars will be at the top of the world: 14,000 feet, with little oxygen to spare and temperatures below freezing. Zico glanced over the corrugated tin roofs of Tambo. At the far end of town, now out of sight, was his family's roof, his home, his mother and brothers, whom he had not seen since that memorable day.

He had had enough.

He looked over his shoulder at the tunnel's mouth, whispered a farewell to his buddies, and headed down. Down, down. From Tambo, high above the world, everything else is down. He was never to go back and never to miss it for a day. Except for *mi familia*, which he carried in his heart with him wherever he went, he had left nothing behind. He always wondered about the fate of his brothers, but above all he cherished the memory of *mi querida mami* (my dear mommy). He had turned his back on the place where girls are born to work and boys are not meant to cry.

He came to a crossroads: a little boy, looking both ways, with no one to help him decide which way to go.

Luxuriant acres of tropical splendor lay toward the sunrise, but Zico now looked the other way. He saw huge Lake Junin spread its smoothness like a mirror far into the west. Like a great magnet it drew him toward the city of Tarma, the Pearl of the Andes. Surely things would be different and better there.

Zico hitched a ride on the back of a truck. In exchange he helped the driver unload his cargo of rice and pumpkins. It was a new feeling to be treated like a normal person. With a quick wave and a "Gracias, señor," he was up and on his way. He now had only a short distance to walk. Streams of melted snow from the heights hurried past on their way to the ocean. Big white puffy clouds changed shapes as they raced into the distance. All of nature seemed to beckon him on his way.

Once again, he grew hungry, very hungry. Yet worse than this feeling — which he had now grown strangely accustomed to — was the terrible feeling of loneliness. Now utterly alone, his only point of refer-ence was himself.

Somehow, in Tarma, he grew to miss Tambo. There were times when he would have gladly traded the dark and noisy alleys of this bigger town for the safety and silence of his old underground home. The simple snatchings of Tambo were child's play compared with the thievery practiced by the more "worldly" street boys of Tarma. Further-more, he never found a friend he could trust. He had burned his bridges behind him. "Why go back, young man?" he now said to himself, mustering up the little bit of humor he still had left. "Ahora todo es adelante" (From now on everything is forward). He smiled. He had surprised himself by what he had just said, but decided to go with it.

From what he had heard, it would seem wise to follow the Palca River toward the land of the Ashaninkas. Most of the waters in this region turn toward the Pacific, but this stream slips into a narrow crevasse between rocks and then plunges through a deep canyon as it begins its long, adventurous journey. It makes its way past Kimo, then grows into a bright, well-behaved river flowing between walls of jungle growth, eventually breaking out into the mighty Amazon to flow unchecked to the Atlantic itself.

But Kimo was not for Zico yet. Only later would he go there to be a living witness to the transforming power of God. He first had to go to Lima, to sink ever deeper into the mire, before being brought out of utter despair.

⁓

Lima was cruel. There was no other word for it. In Tambo, people didn't hurl filthy words at you. And in Tarma, people didn't pull their children to one side and cross the street when they saw you coming. But in Lima, a street boy is not ignored; he is despised. People would rather know him dead than see him alive. Satan seems bent on numbing the senses. He gloats at the tragedy of eyes that don't see and hearts that no longer feel.

Zico's life became a torment. He lived in permanent fear of the police. He was not only thrashed but severely beaten by them, and he witnessed boys who were stripped naked before having water thrown over them and electric wires put to their testicles.

Christmas Eve was the hardest night of his life.

He was not mistreated or insulted. It was worse than that: he was totally ignored. After all, who could possibly care about a miserable boy like Zico? It was a time to celebrate, a time to be jolly. Had he not witnessed for weeks now the mounting excitement over the coming holiday season? All the talk had been of love, of peace, of joy and happiness, all of which Zico had long since repressed. Most painful of all were the references to families, to mothers and fathers, to brothers and sisters and cousins.

When the big metal doors were pulled down that night and the lights were turned off in the store windows, when the last of the busy shoppers were homeward bound and the blast of the joyous music was silenced, the city was as it was most other nights. But not for Zico. He buried his head in his crossed arms and cried for *mami*.

Then came the turning point in his life. He was picked up and brought to Girasoles, Scripture Union's center in Lima for street boys. At first Zico was apprehensive. He toyed with the idea of leaving. Might this be a ruse? Might it be a trap? For the time being, however, he would stay.

When some time later the body of a boy who had been staying at the Girasoles Center was brought in, lifeless, and laid on the dining room table, Zico learned a lesson. What was different was not that another abandoned boy had been shot in the streets of Lima, but the way in which these "big people" reacted. He saw that they were sad. He saw the respectful way in which they treated the body. Above all, noticed the way Susana cried. She wasn't the boy's mother. She owed nothing to a street boy. She had no reason to care. But she cried nonetheless. In the days to come, Zico — now twelve — would find a *mami* in Susana, a human being to whom he mattered and, above all, a friend who would point him to Jesus.

"No greater love has any man but that he lay down his life for a friend," Susana told him on that day.

"Would Jesus really do that for me?" Zico asked, afraid of the answer, but eager to hear it.

"Not only would he," said Susana, "he did."

Most street boys tread a far longer path before accepting the Savior's extended hand, but Zico reached out immediately in faith.

He filled his lungs with the most wonderful air he had ever breathed. His heart beat more lightly than ever before. He must hold this sense of cleanliness and never let it go.

"Would you like to go to Kimo, Zico?" I asked. "Over the top, past Junin, through Tarma, and down the gorge? How about it?"

Zico's face broke out in a contagious smile.

"I'll tell you what," I continued. "I'll take you over with a work team from abroad."

"Gringos (foreigners)?"

"Yes. Twenty-five of them. All Christians. They would like to meet you and hear about your love for Jesus."

"¿Cuándo vamos?" (When do we leave?) he responded, jumping to his feet.

That first night at Kimo, Zico walked out to a rock overlooking the big river. It was still warm from the heat of the tropical day. He stretched out on it. His cheek touched the rough surface. The same stars he had looked at as a little boy were now tangled in the branches of the high jungle trees. He lay there a long time, quietly.

Then: "Thank you, Jesus," he whispered. "I am no longer alone."

3

NANCY
Into Worlds Unknown

*L*ittle Nancy sat alone near her home in the high Andes, pulling the petals out of a bright yellow *retama* and dropping them very deliberately into the narrow stream. As they floated away, she would talk to them, one by one: "How far will you get? I bet not beyond that big stone. You'll be like Mama. And you? I bet you'll get all the way into the big river, like Papa. You might even see the mine he digs in."

She looked past the Mantaro River to the distant mountain range beyond. She dropped another petal into the stream: "Lucky little flower," she mused. "You'll go and go and go. Nothing will stop you. You'll never look back. You'll be taken into worlds unknown. Perhaps beyond the great mountains into the deep, dark jungle." She laughed. "The flowers will all beg you not to go, but they'll never stop you. There's something different about you."

The eight-year-old popped out of her daydream and skipped on home.

Nancy was always different. Mature for her age, she was a Sunday-school teacher at the age of fourteen. She always seemed happiest in the company of older people. She often discussed with them where God might lead her. Although she was basically shy and retiring, there was always a fire within.

She completed her schooling and followed her older brother into the jungle. One by one the entire family joined them. Terrorism was rampant in the mountains and the move made sense, though not for long. Sendero Luminoso (Shining Path) found the Kimo area most suited to their immediate plans. By then there were no safe places left to migrate to, so Nancy's family stayed put.

She started training as a nurse and in her free time made trips deep into the jungle. Her love for Jesus and her passion to live for him grew by leaps and bounds.

This all coincided with Scripture Union's search for a new leader for Kimo. A single man was our first director there. He couldn't handle the jungle. Then came a married man and his family. Looked great on paper, but fear quickly drove them out. Nancy Franco was suggested. What? A shy little mountain lady? She seemed more of a mismatch than David was for Goliath. Yet like the little petal in the stream, she was to go a long way. Nothing would stop God's choice for Kimo.

The following describes an experience that changed the young Nancy's life forever.

There were about twenty Christian families in the town of Satco, forty miles from where Nancy lived, and they had been having a rough time. They met in a little church, but had no pastor. They would by now be needing a bit of encouragement.

"I might not be that good for this sort of thing," thought Nancy, "but I am decidedly better than nothing." She was combing her long, jet black hair and looking in the mirror. She put on that determined look of hers. "Yes, you can do it. You are a strong woman!" She laughed out loud, then added, "Nancy, Nancy, grow up girl."

Out in the kitchen her mother leaned against the plastic raincoats hanging on the wall beside the wood-burning stove. She was fanning the smoke out of her face with one hand and pointing a finger at her favorite daughter with the other. "Nancy, you know better than to go to Satco. If your father were here, he wouldn't let you go. You know that." She poked at the fire with a long stick.

Conveniently for Nancy, a new puff of smoke blocked her from her mother's view. She could now say what she had to say without facing her mother's glare.

"You told me to pray about it, and I have. You taught me that if I did this, the Lord would guide my every step and would never lead me astray. Why can't you trust him now, Mother?"

The smoke had been replaced by the delicious smell of the fried yuca. The old lady sat down on the rough, crudely axed board that served as a bench. She reached across the little table and held her daughter's hand. "Go, my child," she said ever so slowly. "You are right. If you have heard his voice, you must obey."

With that, she walked over to the far side of the stove, replaced the skillet with a pan of water, and filled two plates with the lightly fried yuca. Soon the coffee would be ready and breakfast would be complete.

Nancy and her mother then had a good, long conversation. They hadn't done this in a long time and it felt so good. Except for the occasional lizard and Ceniza, the cat that never took her eyes off them, they were alone. The fact that her father wasn't there made it so much more relaxed. He was a good man but completely lacking in social graces; he somehow always managed to get in someone's way.

They talked their way through all the yuca and countless cups of coffee — good Chanchamayo coffee, the best in Peru, grown right there in and around Kimo. They talked about everything. They even talked about Satco, the great needs there, the dangers on the road, God's protection. Nancy was ready.

Early the next morning, her mother saw her onto the bus. Nancy waved as the bus pulled out, but her mother was quickly enveloped in a cloud of dust. She got off two hours later at the Pumpuriani Bridge. Crossing a high swinging bridge is always an adventure, and Nancy was happy when she was on the other side and safely boarded on the back of a truck. Other passengers, plus goats, dogs, and a chicken or two, were on their merry way to Manco, a town on the Pachitea River. At times it would have been faster to walk, but by late afternoon the truck had made it all the way, and Nancy was happily settled in the home of Carmen, a good friend and traveling companion.

It was a Thursday evening. Nancy asked Carmen to come along with her to Satco.

"Tomorrow's Friday, Nancy, and you know I can't get off teaching school that easily. If you wait for a day, I'll come with you on Saturday. Jaime, my brother — remember him? — can come along with us, too."

Nancy did remember Jaime, who would be eighteen by now. Of course, he could come along, not that he'd do much good. "Sure," said Nancy, "He can even carry our bags!"

Both girls laughed. They knew Jaime, all right.

Nancy helped with the chores around the little two-room house. Everyone slept in one room and did everything else in the other. Actually, most time was spent outside. They were in the steamy jungle and they didn't know what the word "cold" meant. The forest was open and free to anyone.

Late Friday night everyone was probably asleep, but not Nancy and Carmen. The thinnest beam of moonlight slipped between palm fronds and right onto the *tarima* (raised platform) where the girls lay.

"Nancy," Carmen whispered, "are you still awake?"

"Yes," said Nancy. Then after a long silence, "Why? What's on your mind?"

"Nothing."

"That's not true, Carmen. I know you. What's troubling you?"

"Well," began Carmen slowly, "what if we met a terrorist on the trail tomorrow? What would we do? What would we say?"

"I don't know what we'd do," was Nancy's instant reply. "As to what we'd say ..." She hesitated, then continued, "I don't really know." Then, after another short pause, she said: "Oh yes I do. Remember that verse in the Bible? Isn't there one that says something like, 'Don't worry about what you will say. When the time comes, I'll put words into your mouth'? Remember that one? Well, that is just what we can do. We won't think about that now. If something happens, I guess we'll just have to trust God for the right words at the time."

Whether Carmen thought that idea to be good or not, Nancy never knew. Soon they were both asleep.

It would be a full day's walk on a very narrow trail the whole way. They would take turns in the lead, but they would have to walk *fila india* (Indian file), one behind the other, through some of the most breathtaking landscape in the world. After bowing their heads, asking God to protect them from snake bite or jaguar on the trail, they were on their way.

It was a beautiful day and the torrid jungle was alive with dazzling colors set free by the bright beams of sunlight flooding down through the tall jungle trees that rose majestically around them. They were surrounded by the plants that provide the dyes the natives use to color their jungle cotton: scarlets, blues and purples, copper oranges and yellows. Branches of fragrant flowering trees arched gracefully across rushing streams.

"This is more than we deserved," Carmen called back to Nancy. Jaime seemed more intrigued by the giant beetle he held than the magnificent views the girls kept drawing his attention to.

Little by little, the valley they were following turned into a narrow gorge. The trail was now high above the river, which was flanked by the dark forest. Only now and then could a ray of sunlight make it through. At Jaime's insistence, they stopped to watch sauba ants that swept past them like a river, bearing parts of leaves and pausing here and there to feed on some unfortunate beetle.

Soon they were down again. It felt a whole lot safer. But not for long.

"Good thing Jaime's with us," thought Nancy, realizing at last why Carmen had brought him along. He seemed so adept at finding the rocks that could serve as steps up one side of the gorge and down the other. They leapt from boulder to boulder down the ravine.

"Hey, you're young but once," shouted Jaime. Both girls laughed. He was right. It actually was fun. For a while.

"All good things come to an end," he said a bit farther on as the trail reappeared, heading what looked to be straight up. "Why doesn't Nancy, the city girl, take the lead?" he chided. That was all the encouragement Nancy needed.

She was in front for longer than she bargained for. The trail now led higher and higher above the stream and ended up in a narrow ledge roughly hewn out of the cliff wall. Nancy had forgotten this part.

A vertical cliff rose above them on one side and another dropped straight off on the other. The trail was now so narrow that one slip would be fatal. Any beauty still around was now wasted on the travelers.

Behind Nancy came Carmen, and Jaime was last. There were now sharp bends on the trail. At times you could scarcely see ten or fifteen feet ahead.

Around one more hairpin bend, there they were. Two terrorists. Shining Path. Each with a machine gun. Face to face. No space to pass each other.

"Where are you going?" demanded the first man. He was not old, but gaunt and weathered. His hair was scruffy and he wore a dirty purple cap. But all this was lost on Nancy. All she could see were his piercing little eyes.

"To Satco," Nancy barely managed to say.

"And what, may I ask, do you plan to do there?" he said, as though talking to a ten-year-old.

"We are going to talk to children."

"Talk to children? Talk to children about what?"

"About Jesus," replied Nancy, fully aware that this man, like all Senderistas, would be an avowed atheist.

"And what is that going to do for them?"

"He'll change them. Make them better people."

"Change them?" he now thundered, drawing his eyes even closer together. "Only Communism will change them, and they will be better people only when Sendero Luminoso takes control of this country. Who are you?"

"Nancy. Nancy Franco."

"Let me see your documents. The three of you."

All Peruvians carry documents, but they had decided to leave theirs behind. They didn't want to risk losing them, and furthermore, why would they need them on the trail? Nancy glanced back and said, "Carmen, tell Jaime to pass me the bag."

She reached into the bag and brought out her Bible. Handing it to the man, she said, "This is my document."

Her interrogator was furious. "This is your document? This is the book of your religion."

Nancy's voice was now uncharacteristically clear. Her lips no longer quivered. "A document defines," she responded politely. "It tells you about its owner. This is the only thing I have with me, sir."

"Oh," he said, noticing the increased confidence with which she spoke. "So now you are brave? Well, let me tell you something, young woman. You are not going to Satco. You will never again see Satco." He glanced down at the river at the bottom of the deep chasm. "In fact, you are going nowhere."

He lifted his machine gun and touched it to her chest just below her throat. Nancy knew what was going to happen. One more dead body by the side of a road or lost at the bottom of a gully would be like one beetle less in these parts. He placed his finger on the trigger.

"Please, sir," said Nancy, as calm and collected as she had ever been in her life, "allow me to say just one thing before you do it."

He nodded.

"In less than one minute, I shall be in the place I have dreamed about going to ever since I became a Christian. I will be standing beside the one I most love and the one who most loves me. But when your turn comes to die, if you have not repented of your sin and turned to Jesus, you will surely go to hell." Nancy paused and looked him straight in the eye. "Now, do it," she said.

The gun shook. The man's hand began to tremble. Then, in a moment that seemed an eternity he and his companion pressed Nancy, then Carmen, then Jaime against the rock wall and inched past them.

It was all over. The men were gone and the little band of three walked on. All day they had marveled at the creation; now they had just encountered the Creator.

It was probably near midnight when they arrived in Satco. All was very silent as they made their way first to the village plaza. Something seemed different. Then they realized that right in the middle of the square were the remains of a fire. Driftwood bleached in the jungle sun must have made quite a blaze to leave this amount of coals and ashes. On closer inspection they saw some charred and some still unburned remains of books.

"They are Bibles," whispered Jaime, who had not spoken for quite some time. And he was right.

After what had happened on the road, Nancy was now fully in charge. She felt invincible. She had been snatched from the jaws of death by her "best friend," and she knew it. In fact, she now knew him in a deeper, more wonderful way than ever before. From door to door they went. House by house. She remembered where the twenty Christian families lived. They were all awake. All told the same tale: of the visit of the two Senderistas, of the burning of their Bibles, and of the threat to kill the first person to open the church door the next day.

Nancy begged them to come to church, to stand tall in the face of the Enemy. Every family listened attentively to Nancy's story, but all told her that they would not be seen at church. No one knew who had been left behind in the town as an informant.

The next day Nancy stood alone at the church door. It had been roughly nailed shut. She managed to break it free and, with a final push, she was in. She stood framed in the doorway all morning, waiting for at least one other person to arrive.

There was no sign of life until mid-afternoon, when an elderly Christian lady risked it first. She was followed by one and then another and another. By the time the lamps were lit, the church was filled. Even the doorway was packed.

Nancy came from a church where women do not preach. But guess who preached that night? As she faced the frightened crowd, her mind flashed way back to the bright yellow petal set loose in the little stream. "You'll go and go and go. You'll be taken into worlds unknown, perhaps beyond the great mountains into the deep, dark jungle. They'll never stop you. There's something different about you."

Now she knew who that little petal was.

4

NESTOR AND TINO
Home Safe!

I had always been curious about shrunken heads, ever since, at the age of eight, I saw my first one for sale in a store-front window on Jirón de la Union, Lima's main shopping street.

"I don't know that much about them," my father said in his usual unassuming manner.

But I knew better. He had to know. After all, he had been the first Christian missionary on the upper Maranon where the Jivaros and the Shapras live. I pressed, and he finally obliged.

"Well, Paul," he started slowly.

I was on the edge of my chair.

"After they have cut off the head, they remove the scalp, face and all, from the skull. It is then like a bag which they fill up with hot sand. As it cools it shrinks. Then they fill it up again with more hot sand. They knead it all the time so that none of the features become deformed. Eventually they get it down to fist size. And that's it."

"How do they cut the head off? Why do they do it?"

My father hated talking about this horrific practice. "That's enough," he said.

Enough indeed. It would now be unthinkable to tolerate such trade. Many years have passed since those days. Yet the irony of it all is that some of the people who are now outraged at the thought of such a thing are busily engaged — on the very street where I first saw the shrunken heads — in devising ways to get rid of abandoned street boys.

"Why do you take pictures of such boys?" the wealthy owner of a camera shop asked me a few years ago, as he handed me the photos I'd paid him to develop.

"They are boys at our Girasoles Scripture Union Center," I replied. "We see God bringing about real change in their lives."

"Really," he said with obvious disbelief. "My way would be quicker and simpler. One bullet per head."

Let me tell you of two boys who were in those pictures I had taken, two "angels with dirty faces": Nestor and Tino.

Nestor came to us almost by accident, thanks to the unexpected kindness of a prison guard willing to take a risk for the sake of a child. When a member of our staff went to the boys' prison in Lima to pick up one of our boys and was unable to find him, this guard broke the rules and let him take Nestor instead. When Nestor was safely in Girasoles, we discovered that things like care and safety were so alien to him that he didn't know what to do at first. He was too frightened. He did not talk.

All we could hear in those early days was the sound of a boy building a rage over a life that had taken him from his mother, given him the street for a bed, and finally sent him to prison in order to "keep the streets clean."

For a couple of years Nestor guarded his secret fear and rage, allowing no one into his life. No one, after all, would understand. Was he not the bad boy who was put into the street at the age of six to learn on his own the secrets of survival?

From time to time we witnessed old embers of hatred and resentment leap into flame, yet no one could get through to Nestor. He had learned in the street that everyone has answers, but none that can address a street boy's loneliness and fear. He later would say that his silence was worth more to him than a thousand words.

But on a trip to Kimo, Nestor found a friendship that would teach him to trust.

Tino, like Nestor, arrived at Kimo alone. His best friend, Gerardo, had fled the group when he saw the size of the river they were about to cross on the precarious *huaro* (cable car) and sneaked back to Lima.

Devastated by the loss of his friend, Tino was paralyzed by loneliness, even though he was still surrounded by other boys. Sometimes it's lonelier in a crowd than by yourself on a hilltop.

That first night at Kimo he looked up at the bright sky. Just above the nearest thatch roof he could see it: the Southern Cross, ever so bright. It looked both distant and somehow so near. Just as the arms of the cross intersected at an invisible point, so God had planned that two boys, Nestor and Tino, would encounter each other in such an unexpected place as Kimo. They were to become the best of friends, and God would use that friendship as a stepping stone to entering both hearts.

The next day saw the two little fellows heading out on their own for the high look-out at the camp. It's not that easy a place to reach, but then again, taking risks was second nature to boys such as these. The sheer freedom of the place was bewildering to them. The whole world seemed alive and happy. The bright *chihuaco* bird sat on a high limb looking down on the countless butterflies that fluttered in and out between the giant ferns and yellow *alamandas*. The boys laughed at the funny sounds made by the little green parrots that flew overhead and took great delight in catching *saltamontes*, the long-legged grass-hoppers of the high forest.

By the time they reached the distant top, they had both experienced a world beyond their wildest dreams, and bonded into a friendship that would last for life.

High above Kimo now, they sat on the rustic bench under what was left of the palm roof. They looked down and saw the other boys, hardly bigger than the giant killer ants they had encountered on the trail.

They sat there in silence, enjoying the fresh breeze and hot sunshine. This world was so different from Lima. As they looked down, they saw a wisp of smoke seeping through the thick thatch of the cook-house. That meant fire, but also meant good food.

Though their surroundings were now marked with beauty instead of squalor, the boys themselves had not changed, for change comes from within. They had often heard the phrase "la ropa no cambia al mono" (clothes don't change the monkey). Their fun that day was on the surface. At a deeper level, they were still experiencing the torment of the soul. They were born for it, even as the sparks flew upward. They were, after all, the children of flame.

Tino broke the silence. Only Gerardo knew his story, and he hadn't planned to tell anyone else. Street boys rarely do. But on that day in Kimo, it just happened.

"See this?" Tino said, pulling up his trouser leg. "The man who replaced my father did it."

Nestor saw the deep scar and realized why Tino never wore shorts.

"He used to beat me till I bled. My mother was on my side but that did neither of us any good. Then he threatened to kill me. I knew he would. So did Mother. When she put me out, I didn't understand. Now I do. She had to, to keep me alive. I love my mother. I have never seen her since. Maybe someday I will."

Tino knew that Nestor understood. They both knew that the friendly Scripture Union adults couldn't.

And that is our big problem — our daily struggle at Centro Girasoles, Kimo, and elsewhere. I know that until the pain of these street boys hurts me and their tears make me cry, until their hearts throb in my chest and their fears frighten me, I cannot bring them to Jesus. But they can feel one another's pain, and one another's world. They can bring each other into our care, where together we can find a solution.

Tino continued his story. "I met Gerardo in the streets of Arequipa, at the foot of the great Misti volcano. He told me that life would be much better on the streets of Lima. No one would recognize us and there might even be more food."

"Arequipa, Arequipa," Nestor repeated slowly. "Isn't that far away?"

"One thousand kilometers, high in the mountains, sixteen hours by bus. That's how I came."

"Does it cost a lot?" asked Nestor. "Is it easy to steal in Arequipa?"

"I learned how to steal in Lima, not in Arequipa. I went to the bus station. I saw a lady who looked a bit like my mother. She had full skirts, you know, like all *serranas* (mountain women). She was getting on the bus. I asked her if she would take me. As I was still little, she pulled me up, sat down, and hid me on the floor under her skirt. I never got up once till we reached Lima. I kept thinking of what my new life would be like. I never saw that kind lady again. Gerardo was on the same bus. I don't know how he got on."

Nestor stood up. He stretched and took a deep breath of fresh air, so different from the pollution of the big city. He looked down, then up at the deep blue sky. He saw a large bird with a white breast fly past. The only birds he ever saw in Lima were *gallinazos*, big black ugly vultures that compete with street boys and other hungry people for the garbage.

"We are at the top of the world!" Nestor shouted, unafraid that someone might hear. "I wish I were like that bird. I would fly and fly and fly, I don't know where, but I would fly. Maybe I would fly over Lima, and look down and laugh at everyone." He took another deep breath of mountain air.

"Are you afraid to die, Nestor?"

"No. Are you?"

"No. If I did, I wouldn't have to go back to Lima."

Nestor settled down again and his friend continued. "A man in the marketplace loaned us a big three-wheel cart. Gerardo pushed it through the crowded streets of La Parada and I picked up any pieces of cardboard I could see. At the end of the day we would give it to the tricycle man and he would give us a plate of food. We would keep some of the big cardboard pieces to sleep on. It keeps some of the cold of the pavement from coming through."

"I slept on cardboard, too, when I could find a piece," Nestor said. "Otherwise the *terokal* (glue) would take me so far that I never felt the cold anyway."

Tino then related his lucky moment. "One day between two

cardboards I found three soles, enough to buy three bowls of soup. That same day I saw two small boys my size. I left Gerardo and followed them. I later wished I hadn't. They taught me how to steal. It was easy, and besides a plate of food, I had enough for my *terokal* every night. Just like you, Nestor, I no longer had to stay awake at night and think of Arequipa."

"¿Y la policía?" asked Nestor.

"I hate the police. They caught me often. Each time they beat me and put me back out into the street."

"I hate them, too," said Nestor. "Someday I want to be a policeman. That way no one can beat me. I won't torture boys, though. I'll be different. I'll just direct traffic."

"My worst time," continued Tino, "was when they took me to Comas. They put me into the back of a truck and drove me far into the desert. They dumped me there and disappeared. Fortunately I walked the right way and eventually came to a road. You know that they wish us all dead, but I found my way right back to Jirón de la Union. That is the easiest place to steal watches. That is where I met Martinez. He is the one who told me about Scripture Union and Centro Girasoles. He told me that that was the only place I would ever find where big people are good to boys like us."

"I remember seeing you the day you came," said Nestor. "We called you *carachoso* because you were filthy and covered with sores. Do you remember?"

"No, I don't," said Tino, "but I do remember that I could not believe my luck. Gerardo was there. He gave me a big *abrazo* (embrace). Once the police started letting their trained dogs on street boys, he wondered if he would ever see me again."

"What's that?" said Nestor loudly, and with one jump was well away from the lookout.

Tino looked up and saw the same tarantula. They continued their conversation a good distance away.

Tino asked, "Were you there the day Manolo beat up that man in the restaurant?" Manolo was everyone's hero.

"No," said Nestor, "but I heard about it. Tell me again."

"Well, I had washed a car in the Girasoles parking lot, and with the money I went into the restaurant next door and ordered rice and beans. I had just started to eat when this big man stood up and shouted, 'What is this little street rat doing in this restaurant?' Then he hit me across the head. I fell off the chair but quickly got up. 'I know what I'll do,' I thought. 'I'll get Manolo.' So I went for my big brother. Do you call him your big brother, too?"

"Yes, we all do," said Nestor. "So then what happened?"

"I pointed the man out to Manolo. He was bigger than our big brother but not nearly as strong. Manolo pulled the big man up off his seat and said, 'Did you hit my little brother? He's not a street rat,' and gave him a punch that sent him sprawling over the table."

The two boys doubled over in laughter.

"It looked like the movies," said Tino. "We calmly walked away. The owner rents the restaurant from Scripture Union, so he couldn't say anything. Furthermore, he's our friend. Someday I'll be like Manolo," he concluded.

Nestor stood up. He was the best built of our little boys. "But not before me," he laughed as he flexed his muscles.

⸺

On their last night at Kimo, the two sat together at the campfire, across from Carlo, a member of the Scripture Union staff.

"Do you believe what Carlo says about there being a God that cares about people like us?" Nestor asked Tino.

Tino hesitated, then looked up at the sky. Once again the stars were incredibly bright. "When I first came to Girasoles I believed they were lying to me," he said. "They talked about God and about Satan. They said that God was good and that he had created every-thing including the world. But the way they described Satan convinced me that he created the world, our world, Nestor."

Now it was Tino's turn to question. "What would you like, above everything else, even more than food?"

"I want to learn English, but not more than food. And you?"

"I want to wake up from this nightmare."

"What do you mean? You are awake."

"How do you know? Maybe I'm sleeping."

"No, you're not," said Nestor. "You are completely awake!"

"Just maybe I'm not," Tino said very deliberately. "Sometimes it's hard to tell. Maybe I'm not in Kimo. Maybe I'm just dreaming all of this and everything else that has happened to me since I was little."

After a long pause, Nestor asked a very perceptive question: "When you wake up, Tino, where do you want to be?"

"En cama, junto a mi mami" (In bed beside my mommy).

⌐

Tino's wish was so simple and reflected the dreams of most of the boys. We couldn't bring back his childhood bed or his mommy, of course, but we could offer him the comfort of a clean place to sleep, and, much more than that, the love that comes from knowing God.

Several years have now passed since that memorable trip to Kimo. I thought then and know now that in our sovereign God's great picture puzzle of Creation, there were two spaces of a size and shape that only Nestor and Tino could fill.

Today both boys are in Kawai, a Scripture Union home for

abandoned boys in the Peruvian coastal desert. Still the best of friends, they now sit by the seaside when they compare notes. Tino, the talkative one, now says, "Jesus is my Father. I know that he looks after me." This little boy moved from doubt to trust and traded his nightmare for a dream.

As for Nestor, he is still quiet. Last time I saw him, he was walking to the beach alone, his Bible tucked under his arm. He, too, is home safe.

5

PACO
"They Call Me Rat"

$\mathcal{S}$trange as it may seem, my link to little Paco started in far away Camp-of-the-Woods in upstate New York. My wife, Marty, and I had been invited there by good friends. On the Saturday night that we were there we attended a concert given in the large camp auditorium by Ted Smith, Billy Graham's pianist. From the grand piano on an otherwise empty stage came an incredible display of talent as the artist's fingers flew up and down the keyboard, giving us an evening of the most wonderful music. After much applause, he returned for his encore. And that is the part that I will never forget for as long as I live.

Smith came out and very deliberately sat down on the bench. There was a long pause. Then he raised his right hand and, with one finger, played his final number, "Jesus Loves Me." Played ever so slowly, so quietly, so magnificently. What a stark contrast to his previous renditions! The simplicity and power of his version transcended the complexities of the language of music and spoke directly to our most childlike selves. With a few clear notes, he drew a straight line from God to our hearts.

He left the stage. No one clapped. The lights came on. At first, no one got up. The doors were opened. Then very slowly, one by one, people moved toward the exits. It had been one of those few magical moments in life.

I always remember that moment, the powerful message contained in those few simple notes, when I struggle to show a street boy, who has known only rejection and brutality, the depth of Jesus' love for him.

〜

The week before Paco arrived at Girasoles, we were visited by a policewoman.

"I need your help," said the woman. She was intense and nervous. "I have two street boys in the back of this vehicle. I am in charge of the operation. Would you please take them? I understand this to be a home for the abandoned. I really do need your help."

"I understand your predicament," said Isabel, "but you have to realize that we really can't help you out, because ..."

"Why ever not?" interrupted the officer, obviously not used to having her ideas questioned. "I'm from the Sexta Comandancia and you are in my jurisdiction."

"That's not the point," responded Isabel, unaccustomed to this sudden interest in street boys from the nearby police station. "The thing is that ours is an open door to the street. If we take these boys against their wishes, they'll walk right out the back door. We do nothing to stop them. Boys are not brought in here by force, and they don't remain with us a minute more than they want to. We encourage them to stay. We show them all the love we can, but we never take their freedom of choice from them."

Isabel stopped. She hadn't intended to deliver a speech. It was just her natural reaction to the police, who more often than not are known to mistreat boys.

"Would you allow me to explain?" said the policewoman politely. "As I said, I am in charge of this operation and I have a problem of conscience. I have been given an order by my superior. I am accustomed to obeying orders, but this time I have been given one that I cannot carry out. You see, I am a policewoman, but I am also a mother. I have been told to desaparecerlos."

Isabel knew what that meant. It would not be the first time a boy had been "disappeared" by the police. Her demeanor changed. "Yes, of course," she said, "bring them right in, but remember what I told you about our doors. We'll do all we can."

I saw the boys pass my office window. They were a bit bigger than most and looked more angry than frightened.

Later I asked Isabel how she had fared with them.

"They accepted our offer of a shower and food, but then they were gone," she said. She gave me a look I had often seen before, something between disappointment and defeat.

Small wonder we wanted to hang onto Paco when he arrived a few days later.

Paco was a cute little guy, wide-eyed and attentive. His mother, a scantily dressed middle-aged woman, seemed agitated.

Pablo, director of Girasoles, explained that space was limited at our home and that vacancies were filled by boys found living alone in the streets by our staff.

The woman seemed not to listen, but when she spoke, it was clear that every word Pablo said had sunk in. "I'll tell you what you can do then," she said. She leaned forward on her chair, looking first at the boy and then back at Pablo. Poor little Paco couldn't help but be all ears. "Pick him up off the street tomorrow," she said coldly.

"What?" exclaimed Pablo more out of outrage than surprise. "Pick him up off the street?"

"That's right. I will take him right out this door and lose him. Tomorrow you can start looking. Last night was his last night with me."

There was a long pause as Pablo pulled himself together. "So you plan to abandon Paco and force me into feeding him?"

"I'm not forcing you into anything," she said calmly, "nor do I expect you to feed him. I just thought you might want to." She started to move toward the open door.

Pablo looked at the little fellow in disbelief. Of course he wanted to feed him. He could hardly be part of this boy's agony. Yet he felt torn by twin passions: sheer anger at this woman and love for the little boy.

"What would Jesus do?" Pablo asked himself. Of course he knew, but he could not let this woman off the hook without an explanation.

"May I ask you, lady, why last night was the boy's last night with you?" He made no effort to hide his contempt.

"Yes, it's quite simple. He interferes with my business. He's just too big now."

Pablo understood right away. The woman was a prostitute, and her small room was no longer big enough for the two of them. Paco for seven years had shared one bed with his mother and her countless clients.

The woman left and Pablo took Paco into Girasoles.

We all promptly fell in love with this little kid and busily laid plans for his future. Quiet at first, Paco seemed desperate for attention and readily received any show of affection.

But as time went by, Paco seemed agitated and restless. He began to hint that he might leave. At whatever cost, we could not let this happen, especially after the recent visit of that policewoman. Yet it did. Early one morning he slipped out. No one saw him go. No one was there to beg him to stay.

Just as we had no way of understanding the depth of Paco's fear and heartbreak, Paco couldn't be made to understand the dreams we had for him.

Another setback, another bitter pill. Had little Paco, like many of our other boys, traveled too far too soon? Would he go to the nearby Parque de la Reserva and sleep in the branches of some tree with other boys in order to escape being seen? Probably not. He would be too intimidated by the more experienced boys for that. Most likely he would pay the price of every novice: repeated beatings at the hands of the police. Maybe that would bring him back, or maybe not. Who would ever understand why a boy like Paco, or the two who had been brought in by the policewoman, would trade love and care, food and a warm blanket, for a desperate life in the streets?

It was to be years before we saw Paco again. Poor little guy. He lived with memories that prowled across his mind, his heart, and his life, leaving ugly footprints.

⁓

Lima is huge, disorderly, and hard to figure out. Taxis, trucks, carts, and people jockey for position on the crowded roadways. In the Mercado Central area where Paco ended up, street vendors abound, hawking everything from fried plantains to underwear, from herbal remedies to live pigeons, all in close proximity. Her eight million inhabitants are disconnected, with very little in common. They have roots from all over the place: peasant, Indian, Mestizo, Black, and Asian.

There's *Nivel A*, the rich and powerful upper crust, those who trace themselves back to the Spaniards.

Below them there's a middle class, struggling for survival. Not eligible for government handouts and not anywhere close to the sources of power, they are as spiteful toward street boys as everyone else.

Only the poorest of the poor seem to have a heart for the boys, but then they have no resources with which to help. They are the soil in which the problems of poverty and inequality germinate.

Lima is an ancient city, both proud of and embarrassed about its past. Had there been maps of the world when Moses led his people out of Egypt, Lima would have been on them. When the conquis-tadors arrived and overthrew the Inca Empire in the early sixteenth century, they "founded" Lima, tearing down the Incan Temple to the sun and building a cathedral on the site. They demolished the Palace of Taulichusco and replaced it with the Casa de Pizarro. They came to conquer, a sword in one hand, a crucifix in the other. Paco is racially related to those of native blood who later wrote, "Jesus Christ was brought by the white man to our land to crucify the Indian." Life remains very difficult for the descendants of Peru's original inhabitants.

Nearly five hundred years ago, when the Spaniards first came to Peru, they were blinded by their lust for gold. And gold was plentiful. The Inca saw this soft metal as something useful and beautiful. But more beautiful to them were the sunflowers that decked the high terraces above the Sacred Valley, and more useful by far the llamas that carried loads of potatoes to market and the irrigation canals that brought sparkling water down from the melting snow on the southern ridges of the Salcantay. The peaceful and prosperous life of their great Empire was brought to a sudden halt by the greed and vaulting ambition of a ruthless band of white men seeking the precious treasure.

The search for gold and the cruelty and abuse that have always accompanied it have never left us. Today insult has been added to injury. Not only are peasants forced into the mines, but they are despised and looked down on for being peasants. Sadly, in recent times bad has gone to worse.

As though the poor had not been abused enough, we now have an illicit trade in minors. Children, usually boys, are kidnapped from their homes in the high mountains and taken into the jungle to pan for gold. This primarily occurs on the rivers that border the land of the Machiguengas, many of whom still live in the Stone Age.

Children between the ages of eight and thirteen are lined up with straw-matted sieves across the narrow streams to dip into the water for sand that may hold a flake or two of the precious metal. Young men take turns behind them, cracking their whips and shouting, "¡Sigue, sigue!" (Keep going, keep going!).

The Cuzco and upper Madre de Dios area produces very little food and it is cheaper to bring down more children than to properly feed the ones already there. So as they die, they are buried in mass graves, and more are brought in to work.

Conditions are only slightly better for children in the mines themselves. It is not uncom-mon for seven- and eight-year-olds to work there without a break from five o'clock in the morning until six at night. Their life and that of their parents is rugged and hard, invested in survival and creating wealth for the owners of the mine.

⁓

Paco ended up with three other boys on the streets of Lima, all his size and roughly his age. They would become the closest of friends in the ensuing months, bonded by fear and a common enemy: all big people. They quickly learned that if they were looking for a helping hand, they had better look no farther than their own wrist. Even among themselves the law of the street was to be the same as the law of the jungle: each must fend for himself.

Eventually they found a hiding place. Incredible, yet true, it was situated right off Lima's Plaza Mayor, right under Casa de Pizarro, the presidential palace. Ironically, they were least likely to be caught in this area of maximum security. They were as safe as safe could be.

The tunnel was putrid: dark, damp, and smelly. The only light came from the small hole at its one open end. That led to the Rimac, a small river that brings far too little water to the thirsty city. Once a rocky stream that brought the melted snow and ice down to the nearby sea from majestic mountain peaks through rugged terrain, it is now little more than a modified sewer, collecting all forms of refuse from the towns and villages upstream.

But the Rimac was a lifeline to Paco: water to splash in on dark nights when no one could see, something to look at that didn't threaten him, and a source of food when everything else failed: sewer rats, caught under the old bridge that led to the Plaza Mayor. "They taste like guinea pig," he told me later.

Street boys learn from each other, and what they learn shoves them further and further off center. There are no honest jobs for them. In a city of mass unemployment, who in their right mind would hire a street boy? They must steal in order to eat, and keep one step ahead of the police in order to steal.

Like other street boys, Paco did not fear death. He feared life. Occasionally fortunate enough to have some scraps passed his way by a kind street vendor, he more often filled his little plastic bag with *terokal*, the glue used by cobblers to mend shoes and by boys like Paco to escape.

The boys would regularly drug themselves in order to forget. They would sleep long hours in an attempt to disappear from reality.

The boys lived like this for many months. Paco's mind became a battlefield. Like the sets of toy soldiers he saw for sale along Jiron de la Union, it seemed as though everything and everyone was arrayed against the little group hidden in their unknown and abandoned home under the palace.

Finally, a terrifying incident forced Paco to reconsider street life once and for all.

There was one small hole at the top of the tunnel, covered by a grate. Because the boys often saw the soles of boots on it, they kept a healthy distance. One day a palace guard looked down. Whether he saw a boy, some movement, or just became curious will never be known. Before Paco and his friends knew it, several guards burst into the tunnel. It was dark, and at first in their familiar underground world the boys had the advantage. But the entrance was blocked and eventually all were caught, except for Paco. He managed to slip past the guards while they were clubbing the others.

He ran to the river, gained the other bank, and was gone. He later returned to find the tunnel entrance bricked shut. He had had enough. He ran to a distant part of the city and there decided to come back to Girasoles. He had to run five miles through the sprawling city. Even worse, he was caught on his way by two policemen who took all his clothes off and mockingly told him to keep running.

Paco's return that early summer morning made my day. It was February 10, 1998.

I opened the door and he came running in, naked, filthy, and embarrassed.

"I will never leave again," he called out as he ran.

We gave him new clothes. His matted hair was all cut off. After a bath had removed layers of grime and his first proper meal in years had filled his tummy, we began to see traces of the same little boy who had left us years before.

Kimo would be good for Paco. It was a place that would provide healing. Often, wounds run too deep, memories are too unforgettable. The scars they leave only God can erase.

So here, now, sat Paco on Kimo's lookout under the mango tree. Once again I struggled to tell this poor street boy that Jesus loved him.

Jesus? What did Jesus mean to him? Probably the name of another street boy, or perhaps that dead man on a stick in the cathedral of San Francisco or La Merced or any other of the churches where he and his friends had hidden from the police. Who would want to get too close to him?

Love? To a little boy rejected by his own mother and to whom the word "amor" scribbled on bathroom walls meant sex? There had been plenty of that for him in exchange for a bowl of soup on a cold night.

"Me? Who would want to love me?" Paco asked me. "They call me rat, garbage, piranha, dog."

Explaining Jesus' love would be an uphill battle the whole way for those at Kimo who loved boys like Paco. They would have to look past his many shortcomings and much of the nastiness he had learned on the streets. They would have to forgive him time and time again, even if he never asked for pardon. The grime had been removed, but they would still have to look for the real Paco behind the mask he wore. With the Father's help they would have to see Jesus in him.

Explaining Jesus' love to Paco would require the same magic I witnessed at that concert years ago. But I knew, as I talked to Paco that day, that the Father had done some pretty marvelous things in the past. He could do it again.

6

KIMO
The Best Was Yet to Come

*I*n 1974, Peru's Communist-inspired dictatorship issued a land reform decree and we were ejected from Kimo.

That was it. We were out. We never saw the big hut that Calixto built again.

We assembled in Lima to take inventory. We had lost a campsite built with much sacrifice, but we had come away with twenty-four hammocks, twenty mosquito nets, and several kids born into the Kingdom. We were reminded of Job's words: "The Lord has given, the Lord has taken away. Blessed be the name of the Lord." The meeting ended with someone reminding us that God had blessed the latter part of Job's life more than the first. Could we trust God to do the same for us? Could any good really come of this?

We tried to plan our next steps. We waited and hoped.

Then, six months later, came a welcome phone call from Manuel. He had found the new Kimo. And what a beautiful place it was: three hundred acres, all virgin forest, save for fifty that were planted with seventeen hundred productive avocado trees. Right on the big river with two beautiful streams cutting through it. A fairly high, flat plateau surrounded on three sides by amazing forested mountains, right in Ashaninka country. Plus three waterfalls tossed in for good measure. The price was right: $5,000. But there was a problem. It is called *enganche*.

Enganche means "to hook" and it refers to a legal form of slavery, if that makes sense. Here is what we were told: "You will need to *enganchar* about fifteen men to work the avocado plantation. Without them, your prices will not be competitive on the local market and you will fail."

In this system you go to the local bus station and tell them you need fifteen strong, young Quechua Indian men from the mountains where there is hunger and little food. When they arrive, the men are yours and they are in debt to you for the sum of five dollars each — the cost of their bus fare. As long as they remain in debt, they cannot leave your employ. You then give them each a small piece of land to plant their yuca. You supplement this with a small amount of other food, a handful of coca leaf to chew, and a daily measure of *aguardiente* (firewater alcohol). This is rounded off with the sexual services of the hired cook and a pittance of a salary that forces them to keep borrowing meager amounts from you. This serves the purpose of keeping them permanently in debt and on your property until you choose to exchange them for new and stronger models.

This, of course, we could not do, and seventeen hundred avocado trees promptly died. But our purchase led to the freedom of the men working on the property. All of them departed except for Ledesma, who stayed with us for many happy years as *huarero*, the captain of the *huaro*. The *huaro* is a simple four-by-six platform with a few metal strips for a cage, suspended by four pulleys that roll back and forth across the 360-foot-long cables spanning the Chanchamayo River. It is the only way into Kimo and riding in it is a thrilling experience.

Our new and final Kimo was slowly built over the next few years in the fashion of an Ashaninka village, as God provided the workers and the resources.

As always, we were never far from danger. The trouble started right away. Manuel welcomed our director of the new Kimo, Marco, and his wife, Carla, with a big bunch of bananas, which he carried into their cabin. As their baby daughter reached for her first banana, a good-sized snake coiled out. Even scarier was the 165-pound otorongo that Ledesma encountered twice in those early days, or Manuel's driving the old Land Rover off a sixty-foot cliff into the river. (Manuel was fine. So, miraculously, was the Land Rover.)

Marco and Carla left, but not before seeing several young people give their lives to Christ. We thought by then that maybe we had been tried enough. Little did we know that our biggest battles were yet to come.

⁓

One day out in the jungle, Manuel discovered five men, dead, with their hands tied behind their backs. The dreaded Shining Path terrorists had hit the area.

In the coming days, no records were kept of the dead or missing. Evangelical Christians were targeted more than any other group. Their offer of new life in Christ was perceived as competing with Sendero, and the heat was turned up on us at Kimo. Countless victims were bound and thrown off the Quimiri bridge just two bends in the river above us, and people were hanged and left to rot on the high cables of the nearby Paucartambo bridge bearing signs that proclaimed, "Death to Whoever Removes."

Manuel came to Lima to beg me not to come over to Kimo anymore. "We cannot count the number of bodies that float past there," he told me. "The minute you get off the bus, you will be followed. It will make it worse for all of us."

By now Manuel had lost his optimism. He sent his wife to live with relatives where she would be safer. As for him, he felt singularly committed to stick with Kimo and risk passage over the highlands every few months to bring news out to Lima and then go back with a few supplies.

For five years starting in 1987 I never went to Kimo and we stopped running camps there. During that time I thought a lot about the place, about Manuel and his family, about Nancy. I recalled the happy days there. I thought of Job, of the gloating of the Enemy and his Brujo allies deep within the nearby forest. And, of course, I thought a lot about God, of his ways with mankind. Of his ways with his children — with me, for example. What could all this be about? In my weaker moments, I asked, "Why are you doing this to us, Lord?" and in my better ones, "I praise you because you have never made a mistake yet and I'm sure you haven't started to with us."

Marty, my beloved wife, was always brave and encouraged me. She knew how much I loved Kimo. We had both put a lot of our lives into it, and God had promised his blessing. She seemed always to remember this better than I, and reminded me of the many people he had brought to himself in that place, in spite of the mounting problems.

But I could never have been prepared for the news Manuel brought when he rang our doorbell at 4 o'clock one morning.

It had been a long trip for Manuel over the top of the Andes in a freezing bus, but you would never know it from looking at him. Calm and collected as usual, he sat down to a cup of coffee. Marty joined us. It was far too early to get excited or upset. Probably a good hour of the day just to feel numb. There was a telling silence. Then ...

"Sendero has taken Kimo," Manuel said. He told us how he had been nailing up some fruit crates on the side of the road to ship papayas to Lima. He had made this his activity just to keep an eye on Kimo from across the river and at the same time not be linked to Scripture Union. Here's the story as he told it to us.

A truck stopped one mid-morning and six terrorists jumped off. "Take us over to Unión Bíblica," one of them snapped.

Surprised, but not showing it, Manuel obliged. Only three could fit on the *huaro*.

"The place is abandoned," Manuel said, as they made their way to the camp.

"We'll believe that when we see it."

"Unión Bíblica has forgotten all about this place. They haven't been here in years," he continued.

The beetles and spiders, termites and cockroaches had all done us a big favor. When they came to the storage room where the mattresses were kept, one of the men ordered him to open the door. It was padlocked.

"I don't have the key here."

"Open the door!"

Manuel turned his pockets inside out. "I'll cross the river and bring the key. You'll only find rat-eaten mattresses, I'm sure."

They didn't wait for the key, but instead kicked the door down. Manuel, for the first time, silently thanked God for rats. Then they moved themselves into Kimo. They used it as a base from which to attack nearby La Merced. Not long after that, I saw in the newspaper that the air force was bombing the right bank of the Chanchamayo River to flush Sendero out. "That's all we need now — a bomb," I remember thinking. I later discovered that they had never suspected Kimo. It would have been an easy target. Their nearest bomb struck three hundred yards east.

The terrorists then left, to come back a second time. After that they left the place for good — in shambles, a near disaster.

But God was not through with Kimo. We weren't ready to concede defeat. Indeed, the very best was yet to come.

7

PEPE
All Taken Care Of

"Your turn," Pepe said, as his friend tried to think of a way out of an impossible situation. Pepe had him cornered. His next move would have ended with the smashing of his rival's glass marble. That's the way the game of marbles is played in this squalid frontier town on the lower Perene: to the finish. But Pepe had a tender streak. "¡Qué bestia!" (What a fool!) he shouted as he deliberately missed on his next turn.

The other boy understood. "Thank you," he said, picking up his marble and heading home.

"Why do we always have to play this way?" Pepe asked himself. "Así es" (That's the way it is), he shrugged, and walked down the dusty road that would lead him past El Profesor's house on his way home.

Everything seemed different these days. People, too. Even Mamá and Papá. They often talked about moving, but all they owned was their little *chacra* where they planted yuca and bananas to eat and a bit of fine Peruvian coffee, which they sold in La Merced. They could hardly take that with them, and furthermore, there was nowhere safe to go.

That dreaded word "safe" kept popping up. Pepe hated to hear it, but he could not figure out why. Somehow whenever the big people gathered, they usually ended up talking about the new teacher at the school. El Profesor seemed to trouble them, but Pepe liked him.

El Profesor was different from other teachers. He was a little enigmatic. He was definitely popular with the big kids, especially the boys. It was true too that as long as you listened to him, he gave you no homework, and the tests were always easy. But, there was something more than that made him different.

By the time Pepe was thirteen, around 1987, life in the village had really changed. Many who could afford to move deeper into the forest had done so. Those who remained had by now taken sides. If you stood behind the government, the armed forces, and the police, you could still feel "safe." But you had best not talk about it openly. The big people no longer gathered to talk about "the problem."

At school the kids all knew far more about what El Profesor called The Cause than their parents did. Sendero Luminoso (Shining Path) was the way to freedom, equality, justice, and food for all, according to the teacher. "Chairman Gonzalo will do for our beloved country what Lenin did for Russia and Mao did for China," he told the students. "There will no longer be rich and poor, landowner and peasant farmer, those who drive cars and eat meat and those who walk barefooted and eat yuca. You must grow up to be brave and courageous: we are still in the first stage."

El Profesor grew more and more confident as he won more and more of the village's youth over to his cause.

Pepe loved his parents and his brothers and sisters, especially Carlos, the oldest. But deep within him the battle raged. How could he be true both to those he loved and those whose cause he had now secretly embraced?

Sendero Luminoso had started high in the Andes in 1980. To twenty million Peruvians, they were violent, ruthless terrorists who posed a real threat to democracy, both in Peru and beyond its borders. By the time their murderous rampage ended in the mid-nineties, they would assassinate some 70,000 hand-picked victims. But to Pepe and his friends, and to Communists worldwide, they were brave and committed freedom fighters.

By the time Pepe turned fourteen, his mind was made up. The boy who so recently had found it impossible to shatter another's marble would now trade his pen for a gun, his youth for an ideal, his family for a cause. But only for a time, Pepe promised himself. Someday his parents would understand. They were dirt poor and he would bring them prosperity. They deserved to be treated decently, and their lot in life would change when justice was done. He would do his part for their sake, and someday they would thank him. There was a price to be paid for his love of them, and he was prepared to pay it.

There would be no farewell, no last words, no parting to look back on. True to what he had been taught, he took nothing for the long trek, burned every bridge behind him, and with head held high walked into the sunrise with never so much as a glance over his shoulder.

At a prearranged point he met up with two other boys, both younger than he, and El Jefe, his new boss, whom he would learn to believe, trust, and follow without reservation.

"Why are you crying?" Pepe asked one of his new companions, whose name was Alfredo.

"Mi mamá, mi mamá," Alfredo blurted out.

The other boy was trembling, too, Pepe saw. Pepe would soon discover that most boys in Sendero had been stolen from their homes. Unlike him, they had not yet been "prepared."

"You will learn from me," said El Jefe, looking toward Pepe, "and they will learn from you. Is that clear?" It was. Everything the boss said was clear, whether you got it or not. "You are no longer boys," he continued, "You are men. You are not young men. There are no old men or young men in The Cause. We are just men. And men don't cry. Is that clear?"

Pepe felt sorry for the other boys, though he knew El Jefe was right. El Jefe had to be right: that's the way it was. Pepe had by now forgotten how to cry, but sometimes he wished he hadn't.

As they continued down the path, Pepe kept his eyes on his leader, yet somehow knew that his heart was being left behind. Alfredo's tears briefly reminded him of the ones he had secretly shed and took him back to the family he had turned his back on, especially Carlos, who had always been his hero.

"Run!" El Jefe's crisp command startled the boys out of their daydreaming. Minutes later, completely out of breath, the four sat protected by the giant root of a capirona tree.

"Even the jungle is full of eyes," began the second lesson of the day. "They are everywhere. Tongues, too. They belong to *soplones*, those who alert policemen or soldiers to the presence of terrorists. They are the voices of the enemy, the ones Karl Marx called the 'bourgeois.' We are the voice of the poor, the exploited."

He hesitated, like a museum tour guide who had lost his line. But he picked up with, "The marginalized are the ones referred to on the Statue of Liberty as 'the huddled masses.' The correct word is 'proletariat.' Learn that word. Proletariat. That is who we are." Then, in an attempt to sound convincing, he added, "And we will someday rule this country."

The talk was over for a while. "Drink, drink," he commanded. "No food today. Just water. Water is our food. Remember that."

They followed their leader for hours that day along what he called a path, but one they could not see. He would later say, time and time again, "Caminante, camino no hay. Se hace camino al andar" (Walker, there is no path. You make a path as you walk).

Over the next few days of walking, running, and hiding, they ate only a bit of yuca and a few bananas. They were constantly reminded that the path was not the object of the exercise. The only object was the ultimate triumph of The Cause.

Over the next two and a half years, Pepe lived a lifetime of rough and often bitter experiences. With the addition of other boys like Alfredo and some older men, the original group of four had grown to sixteen.

Pepe's volunteer status gave him a certain standing but no privileges. Even El Jefe allowed himself none of these. But things would soon change. With the addition of the four who had recently come down from the high Andes and who were seasoned in the art of killing, El Jefe's group was deemed ready.

"The moment of truth has come," he said as he looked intently at the men through the flicker of the candlelight. "We shall all ..." Here he deliberately stopped. Then he started again, only this time louder. "We shall all take part in eliminating the enemy. We shall together take the villages on the upper edge of the Gran Pajonal. Is that clear?"

Of course it was clear, but no one responded. His small, beady eyes seemed to draw together. "Is that clear?" he thundered this time. And this time they all quietly echoed one another in the often rehearsed, "Sí, señor."

Pepe's mind went into high gear, seemingly out of control. A myriad of emotions fought for his attention. Fear prevailed as never before. Yet he would gather himself together before going to sleep. After all, he had been taught often enough how to do this. He would string up his hammock between trees and go over the list for the umpteenth time:

The Goal: power in the hands of Chairman Gonzalo.
The Method: death to the enemy before the eyes of the people.
The Model: China. The Cultural Revolution. A People's Trial.
The Facts: *ONE*. Communism is like a giant wave approaching the beach. Capitalism and its blind followers have no way of stopping its advance. All their bullets, bombs, and hi-tech weapons will go right through, but the great wave of Freedom will move on. Someday it will break and cover the beach. The world will then be a better place.

    TWO. Bullets can never stop a good idea. Communism is an idea. The only thing that can stop a good idea is a better one, and the world has never thought of one better than our Cause.

Pepe was ready. He had survived years of hardship, hunger, pain. His brain had been stretched out of shape, his heart relocated, and his emotions virtually shot. True, there was no turning back — not that he would go, even if he could. He had been singularly committed to The Cause, though he had to admit to himself that he always had harbored certain misgivings. He had never quite managed to silence an ever-so-quiet voice deep inside that hinted of another way.

    An old Ford truck rumbled down the road and stopped just ahead of them. The sixteen men all climbed in, with nothing save the clothes on their backs and a machete. A three-hour drive enveloped in dust brought them through six miles of potholes into the village of

Quesampi. Rarely did a vehicle enter this village, nor had any of the villagers ever seen sixteen men climb out of a truck. But rumors moved more quickly than trucks in these parts. Few seemed surprised at the visit, and even before the men unfurled their hammer and sickle flag, they were recognized as Sendero.

The well-planned attack was carried out without a hitch. In less time than it takes to cook a pot of yuca, all the villagers and their families were herded into the plaza, the main square.

El Jefe, of course, presided over the trial. He and two others had come previously to the village to coordinate with the schoolteacher, so it was easy now to identify the *enemigos del pueblo* (the enemies of the people).

Before the assembled crowd, the owner of the tiny village pharmacy, and Abdias Vilca, the man who owned three more cows and a few more sheep than anyone else, were brought forward.

"Pueblo," exclaimed El Jefe in his most imposing voice, "we have come to do justice. You are here to do justice. You are the People. This is your case, and you will be the judge and give the sentence. We will carry out your decisions."

"This man," continued El Jefe as the pharmacist was placed in a kneeling position before the crowd, "is the one who became rich off your poverty. He is the villain who turned you away empty-handed when you could not pay the amount he demanded for the medicine he prescribed to ease your suffering. It was he who closed up his shop at sunset and refused to open when during the night you brought your fevered children for help. Has anyone a good word to say in defense of the coward who in his senseless rush toward wealth condemned your little ones to die?"

Needless to say, no one said a word. Everyone knew the fate of anyone who spoke up for the accused at a People's Trial.

Then a similar scene took place for poor Abdias Vilca, accused of turning a blind eye to those less fortunate than he.

Pepe could not sleep that night. He couldn't get the images of the executions out of his mind. He had never before seen anyone chop two heads off with their machetes. He didn't sleep and threw up twice. Could this really be the way forward? Was it right? Might the way of Mamá and Papá, which he had willfully rejected, be the right way after all?

"Shame," Pepe shouted as he jumped out of his hammock, waking Alfredo. "I just had a shameful thought. I should know better." And he rushed over for the big breakfast the men had been offered.

Every trial ended with taking away all the belongings of the ones whose bodies were left, under orders, to rot in the public square. This meant food and drink and a welcome break in the long "training march."

Then came Pepe's turn.

"It's never easy," said El Jefe. "Not the first time, I mean. After that, it is."

Pepe knew what his leader was talking about. He had always dreaded the moment, but knew it must come. He was ready. He would not flinch. He must remember that the final prize makes every price worth paying.

Pepe had not spoken a word, but El Jefe could read his mind. Had he not had similar thoughts, way back, now long forgotten? For the first time ever, the older man showed a gentler side. He put his arm around Pepe. "Boy," he said, "I'll be with you. I will do it. You be my assistant. Then next time you'll be strong enough to do it yourself."

Only one execution this time. The man brought forward was perhaps in his mid-forties. His wife and three little children stood behind him, at El Jefe's command. With a sea of expressionless faces as a backdrop, El Jefe made the usual accusations. Pepe didn't recall the details this time. Did it really matter?

Alfredo handed Jefe an axe. Two others held the accused man and bared his chest as he kneeled before Pepe. El Jefe grabbed Pepe's arm and drew him close. "Follow my orders," he whispered. He raised the axe and with one blow split the man's chest open. Then he squeezed Pepe's arm and gave him his orders.

Pepe obeyed: he reached into the man's chest and pulled out his still-beating heart.

This was the moment that would haunt Pepe forever.

At the age of eighteen, his body was ravaged by tuberculosis and his soul consumed with fear. He could now barely keep up with the group. But as usual, he gave it his best effort. After all, for him there was only one way, and that was forward. His commitment to Communism was his life, and his comrades surely would be the last to let him down. Had he not heard, so many times, "One for all and all for one"?

That's what he thought until the morning he couldn't get out of his hammock. El Jefe came over, looked him in the eye, and said bluntly: "Pepe, you are ill and worn out. You are of no future use to us. We must keep moving. You can go home."

The man turned around and headed off briskly after the others who had gone ahead down their shining path. Pepe lay there, stunned. Later, recalling that moment, he said he had felt like an orange with all its juice wrung out, thrown in the garbage heap.

Pepe went home.

Years before, when he had first left, his parents were deeply troubled. Over time their sadness had turned from disappointment to anger and finally to indifference. He would now be allowed back into the house, but would never be welcome there. Mamá and Papá would never again see him as anything but a disgrace to the family.

But there was one big exception: Carlos. He, too, had grown to hate the memory of his younger brother. But something big had recently taken place in his life. He had given it to Jesus Christ. Love for his wayward brother had been one of the signs of the Spirit's work in his life. He rushed to greet Pepe, who was now taller than he, and gave him a very big hug.

"Bienvenido a casa" (Welcome home), followed by: "You have no idea how happy I am to see you. I talk to God about you every morning."

If this talking to God every morning business had been beyond the family's understanding, it was totally beyond Pepe's. He recoiled from the embrace. "Religion is the opium of the people and God a figment of your imagination," he said. "There is no one to talk to in the morning, at least not for me."

Carlos knew where his brother was coming from. After all, he had gone to the same school and had heard El Profesor's endless speeches. But the older brother knew what he was about.

"I was going to travel south, Pepe, but now that you are here, I have decided to stay. Every morning I will read to you from God's Word and tell you about Jesus. I love you so much, Pepe, that I will not rest until I see the Good Shepherd take you up in his arms."

And that is exactly what happened. In due time, Pepe gave what was left of his shattered life to the Master.

A short time later, Pepe was welcomed to Kimo by Nancy for what was to be one of the most amazing camps ever held by Scripture Union.

You must understand that no inconvenience in Peru was ever much of a problem, certainly not in those troubled days.

Kimo could only accommodate fifty people, and that day eighty young people showed up. The place had been ransacked by Shining Path terrorists and left in desperate need of repair. The heavy rains had caused a landslide, and the water supply was limited at best. Still, "No es problema" was the prevailing attitude.

The camp was to last all twenty-eight days of February, and nothing had been planned but Bible studies. Far from being a problem, this is why so many young folk had decided to come, taking a risk or two for the Kingdom.

Up at dawn. Time for a private encounter with God. Breakfast and wash-up. Bible study right through the morning. Lunch and wash-up. Bible study all afternoon. Supper and wash-up. Evening meeting and testimonies. Then to bed.

Every day for twenty-eight days. No variations on the theme. No hikes, no sports, no recreation. And what's more, no one wanted hikes or sports or recreation. Life was no longer about playing, death no longer reserved for the elderly and the infirm. Too many Christians had recently been killed to make churchgoing fashionable. Not that it had ever really been fashionable. The difference now was that it singled you out publicly as a follower of Jesus and set you up as a target. Needless to say, no one came to a Scripture Union camp or to Kimo for safety or fun. They came out of a need to know God better.

"Pepe bloomed like the tall and majestic palo rosa tree in summer," Nancy would say later. "Every day there was change in him. The old leaves dropped off one by one as the life of the Spirit flowed through him like new sap through branches now fresh and bright."

Pepe had a lot to sort through. He had, after all, lived through more in the last few years than most people experience in a lifetime. He was allowed to break away from the group every now and then. The leaders knew that Pepe needed to talk to someone. He found the right person in Nico, one of our staff who had traveled to Kimo for this special camp. Nico knew how to listen and was always sensitive to God's prompting in the use of his Word.

Pepe would come back time and time again to the incident that had deeply scarred his spirit and had traced itself indelibly on his memory. "I will never forget. I can never forget," he would say, and then stop.

"Go ahead, Pepe," Nico would say. "Tell me again. Tell me as often as you want to. I need to hear it again."

"I will never forget," he whispered loudly. Then he tried once more and this time managed to say, "I will never forget what it felt like to feel the heart of that man still beating in my hand."

Then he would break down.

Nico would put his arms around the boy. "Pepe," he would say, "God has forgiven you. Remember that verse? 'As far as the east is from the west, so far has he removed our sins from us.' When God forgives, Pepe, he forgets. He really forgets."

Pepe would look up and say, "Pray, brother Nico."

"Our Father," pleaded Nico, "keep reminding Pepe that you don't know what he's talking about. Amen."

After a long, thoughtful pause, Pepe would break into a big smile. "It's all taken care of, right, brother Nico? He's forgotten."

"You got it, boy. All taken care of."

8

CÉSAR
Between Silence and Sound

$\mathcal{A}$mazonian water turtles seem to have a touch of romance. They come up onto the sandbanks on moonlit nights eager to deposit their eggs. They dig a hole with their hind feet, lay their eggs, cover them up with sand, and plod back into the river.

Turtle eggs are a staple for many who live in the Amazon. In many tribal groups, though, expectant parents refrain from eating them out of fear that their children will be born mentally deficient.

I wish that our poor little César could blame turtle eggs for his mental slowness, instead of the real cause: a family that beat him constantly from the time he was an infant. Countless blows to the head did the damage that César will live with for the rest of his life. Perhaps it's fortunate that he remembers very little from his past. He is spared some of the pain of looking back in anger.

Young César was finally put out of his family home for being a useless burden on them. On that day, he would trade one form of abuse for another: his family's violence for the danger and misery of life on the streets of Puerto Belén, a slum outside Iquitos.

Belén, on the banks of the Amazon over two thousand miles upriver from the sea, is a place unequaled anywhere in the world for filth, disease, and squalor. The raw sewer of the city spills right into its waterways. Recurring epidemics of cholera and typhoid fever wipe out entire segments of its population. Vultures vie with children for food in the garbage heaps.

On the brighter side, the sun always shines, it is never cold, and the river will never dry up. Canoes are plentiful and dugouts have no parts to wear out. Even if cooked in river water, plantains are good and there is always the hope of catching a fish. As everywhere else, in Belén happiness is a choice, and rather than look at the cloud, most people choose to see the silver lining.

From September to December, when the rivers are low, Puerto Belén was a good place to hide. There César could feel safe along with other boys who also had been ejected from their homes and abandoned. But even there César was at a disadvantage because of his damaged brain. He was slower than the rest. He rarely could follow the plan, was clumsy when it came to snatching food in the market or watches on Calle Próspero, and couldn't make friends. He was regularly set up by the group he was running with to be caught by the police.

"Una raya más no le hace nada al tigre" (One more stripe does nothing to change a tiger), the saying goes, and so another beating by the local police would do nothing but add one more line to his résumé.

Most of the year is rough, but there is always the anticipation of Carnival, the week before the forty-day Lenten period that ends with Holy Week. Sadly, though, Holy Week in Belén is relegated to Good

Friday only. Jesus is taken off the cross, paraded in a coffin through the town, and then put back up on his cross again — always dead. That's it. As for Lent, what more is there for Belén residents to sacrifice?

Carnival is a week of "anything goes," with rules and regulations tossed to the winds. "Eat, drink and be merry, for tomorrow we die" is the theme of Iquitos during this time. There may not be much eating in Belén, but *aguardiente* (firewater alcohol) and promiscuity are the order of the day.

It was a week after Carnival in 1979 when I first took my son Billy to Belén. He was thirteen. He knew Kimo inside and out, and now I wanted to take him on a trip deeper into the jungle.

The waterways were busy. Canoes jostled for position as they crisscrossed around the city. We sat in the middle and back of the narrow dugout that we had hired for our little tour. Andres, the owner, was a pleasant young man, and he rowed from the front as people do in these parts. Snap, snap, Billy took pictures and all was well. Pictures, after all, don't record the smell, and we didn't have to touch the contaminated water. Or so we thought.

Above us, high on stilts, two street boys doubled over with laughter. For them Carnival was obviously not over. They had thrown a large pot full of urine and excrement over us. Billy bristled. The boys were his age, and he was ready for a fight.

Andres calmly paddled on. He would later wash off right there in the canal. We were not in a frame of mind to wash off one lot of sewage with another. I calmed Billy down, and we thanked and paid our boatman and set off for our hotel.

That night, with fresh clean clothes on, Billy and I sat in comfortable seats on our flight back to Lima. As he slept, I sat there, lost in thought. As I look back on that night, I now believe that God was there, prompting me.

Why had those boys done that to us? Then I remembered that there are very few things in the life of a street boy that bring relief from fear and anger. This had undoubtedly seemed fun and funny to them. I wondered what Jesus' reaction would have been. Paddle on, ignoring the act and the actors as I had done? Or stop to change the life of those poor kids?

"Well, I'm not Jesus," I mumbled to myself. But that night on Aero Peru this smug answer was not good enough. I felt that Scripture Union should establish a center for street boys there in Iquitos. I shared my dream with the board, but they turned it down. It was not the first time, after all, that I had been told that the Movement could not keep pace with the speed of my dreams. So just a few of us decided to pray, and we did so for ten full years before the first move was made. We soon found our ideal staff in bright, enthusiastic Samuel, and in Noemi, a bundle of high energy with a limitless store of love and compassion.

But there was one important piece missing, a person emotionally equipped to meet boys in streets and alleys and hiding places. Someone with the most difficult gift: instant rapport.

It was then in God's providence that I met Juan Dávila, a man ideally suited to the task. Juan had been a street child himself. Who better to understand a boy who cries and has no one to care for him, who shouts out in the silence of the long night and hears only his own echo in response? Like César and the other boys, Juan had grown too old too soon. He would understand a boy whose sun was setting before it ever fully rose. He was to be God's choice in telling these boys that Jesus "knows the feelings of our infirmity" and in leading them to faith in him.

His testimony was simple. An emotional man, he always told it with tears in his eyes. "When I was seven, I was chased out of my home with a kitchen knife. I started running and never stopped until at the age of nineteen I met Jesus."

In those twelve long years, he had made his way through three hundred miles of desert, over the towering Andes, and deep into the jungles where rivers flow east. He had lived for five years at the beck and call of a middle-aged prostitute who fed and clothed him in exchange for his services. His emotions had withered up and he had become cold and cynical. Life, at best, would be for him nasty, brutish, and short.

Or so it seemed, until that memorable night on which he drifted into a little evangelical church, heard a Bible message that he later could not remember, and was transformed by the grace of God. As long as he lived, Juan would never for a moment doubt his salvation.

Later, looking back over his life, he felt compelled to find the woman whose bed he had shared as a boy. After a lengthy search, he found her in a village nestled in the high mountains of Peru. She was old, worn out, and bitter. Juan pled with her to accept God's pardon, but his words did not penetrate so hardened a heart. The last thing she said to him as he left her house was, "Juan, my boy, thank you for coming, but for me it is now too late."

Juan, the grown man, saved by the power of God, left the tiny village and cried his way down the hill. But before he got home, he would determine to spend the rest of his life reaching out to boys for whom it was not too late.

So it is not surprising that God put Juan in our way. He joined Samuel and Noemí, and our staff was complete. We were ready to go.

César came in that first day with several other street boys to inaugurate our feeding program. He was the first of many to whom we showed love by allowing them space on the floor where they could sleep at night.

César is not an easy boy to work with, or to help, for that matter. We must fill in all the blanks he leaves empty when he tries to communicate. We must try to understand the subliminal messages in his awkward speech. Finally we must interpret God's word to him in that place between silence and sound. Surely God, who saved Juan Dávila through a message he could not remember, could do the same for this mistreated boy.

As the days went by, César would hesitatingly share just a bit of his past with Juan.

I remember the time, some months later, when César begged to have his picture taken. He was fifteen by now, yet had never been photographed. I agreed, and in return I asked him to show me where he slept when he didn't sleep at the center.

We walked to the Cementerio General. It was surrounded by high walls. The big gates were open during the day but locked at night. I asked him how he got in. He showed me some gouged-out holes in a remote part of the cemetery's brick wall on Calle Bolognesi.

"I go over here," he said. "The night guards know me and don't kick me out." He showed me where he slept. It was on the ground beside his grandmother's grave. "She loved me," he whispered. "She is the only one who ever loved me. I want to sleep beside her."

We walked on quietly, he with his thoughts, I with mine. We walked past the *fosa común* (deep hole), where the fire never goes out. The place for the bodies of those whose families cannot afford a burial. And, of course, for throwaway boys like César.

I took the photo. "God," I prayed, "break into the life of this dear boy. Tell him that you love him."

We were only three blocks away, yet it seemed a long way back to our center that day.

César often comes by. He also wanders around the town. Sometimes I see him down by the river in Puerto Belén when I take Christian visitors from abroad who have come to assist us in our ministry. As we walk or canoe around, we often pass one or another little evangelical church, mostly up on high stilts. As for César, he paved the way for many street boys to come to us. I sense, in his distant and ever-confused smile, the reality that he has seen God. I know that God has seen him.

9

LUIS LUNA
The Boy Who Lived Again

"¡Lárgate!" (Clear out!), the man shouted as he pushed seven-year-old Luis through the door. "No te quiero ver más" (I never want to see you again). The child looked right past the angry man and into his mother's tearful eyes. All too often he had heard her arguing and fighting in his defense. This time it was different. She didn't call him back. Instead, she waved goodbye.

He cried, then began to tremble. He looked all around. There was no one left for him. His mother was all he had. He was terrified. Where could he go? He had seen abandoned boys before. He would have to find and then follow them. Yet maybe, if he waited, his mother would come out. He stood behind a big mango tree and gently rubbed his hand up and down the rough bark. He picked at it nervously as he mounted his useless vigil. Night came, but his mother never appeared.

He fell asleep that night beside two street kids who allowed him to lie down with them but would not give him their names. He awakened when a mangy dog licked him. He was alone. The other two had taken off. He would later learn that in the streets of Pucallpa on the banks of the upper Amazon it is far better to stick it out alone. When he woke up a second time, even the dog had moved on. Fortunately he did not realize, when he saw the sun shimmering on the pavement ahead, that his road would be a long one to follow and that he was to spend the next nine years chasing mirages.

He found a soup kitchen. "What's your name?" asked the grumpy woman.

"Luis."

"Luis what?"

"Luis Luna."

"Where do you live?"

Silence.

"Where do you live, boy?" she demanded.

Silence.

This is how Luis learned that soup kitchens don't serve street boys. What was even harder to take, though, was that he never found another boy willing to throw his lot in with him, share a sidewalk with him, or search a dumpster with him. As with all but the lucky few who found someone to trust in, Luis was destined to live alone.

Other boys had convinced him never to look for his mother. "Once you have been put out," they all assured him, "there is no return for a piraña."

He had always known the *piraña* to be a little fish in the big river. Sometimes when there was nothing better to be had, people ate them. Otherwise they were just tossed back in. They were nasty little fellows, ugly and worthless, best left alone. At first he didn't get the connection.

Luis didn't want to stay in the streets of Pucallpa for long. It was too big a town, too busy. Furthermore, he might run into the man who had pushed him out of his home — or his mother, for that matter. But it was his first encounter with the police that caused him to flee the city in terror.

He and two older boys had been caught stealing, and he found himself waiting in a police station. Luis had heard terrible things about the police. "Don't ever get near one of them," his father had always cautioned him. "They are all the same, a damned lot!" And he should know. His father had lived beyond the borders of the law: Luis had more than one scar to prove it.

As Luis waited, he heard the other boys scream in the room they had been taken to. He cried as he sat looking up at the image of Santa Rosa of Lima on a shelf on the wall. She was surrounded by old and dusty plastic roses that contrasted with her candlelit face. "If only she would come down," he thought. But, of course, she didn't — any more than did the other Santa Rosas he was to see in many other police stations.

He himself was lucky that day. He and the other boys were tossed back out into the busy street and each ran off his own way.

Luis' way led down to the river. He had been there before. He always liked seeing the big riverboats come and go, and the countless smaller boats and canoes, too. Men carried sacks of grain on their backs down the planks and ran back up, the muscles in their legs bulging as they carried heavy loads of long green bananas, secured to their foreheads by a wide burlap strap. *Patrones* (boat owners) vied with one another for the attention of passengers, each eager to fill up his boat and move on downriver. The space left by one departing vessel was instantly filled by another.

Farther up the bank, the activity was no less feverish. Wholesalers got rid of the larger loads while arriving passengers sold the smaller amounts they had brought from their jungle clearings. These included pigs, ducks, and many chickens. They all hawked their items, creating a spectacular noise augmented by food vendors trumpeting everything from fried yuca to turtle liver soup.

Luis was hungrier than he had ever been before. He hung around and found an overripe banana on the ground. That would do. He ate it along with a piece of yuca one of the vendors gave him. He wandered toward the river's edge and heard a tall man in a green shirt call out to him: "Sube chico, sube" (Get on, kid, get on). Without a second thought, he moved up the long plank and onto the narrow, littered deck.

"Wow," he thought, with a mixture of surprise and excitement. "I wonder where we are going?" Before he knew it, they were off. To Luis, it didn't really matter where. What difference would it make anyhow? He was glad to see Pucallpa fade on the horizon as La Gaviota eased around a bend and headed into the sunset.

The man in the green shirt came by and said, "Sit down here in the corner, chico. From here you have a good view of the river. Later you can lie down. In the morning we'll be in San Benito. When you see the passengers line up for food, look for me. Then you can sleep. These people all bring mosquito nets, but you don't really need one. The breeze on the open river blows them all away."

And with that, the kind man was on his way.

When the kerosene lanterns were all turned off, the last of the passengers climbed into their hammocks. Young Luis, with his tummy full, curled up in his corner for the best night he'd had since he left home.

For the next six years it was to be the same story, one boat after another, one town and then the next. Thieving, running, snatching, hiding. Countless encounters between the men in uniform and the boy who grew taller and thinner, older and angrier at a world that passed him by. Up and down the King of Rivers and in and out of its myriad tributaries, the silent highways of the jungle. A world where men blowgun squirrels and eat them. Monkeys, too. But hardly a place for a boy who had lost his way and all recollection of his childhood dreams. A boy who found it easier to run than walk, safer to hide than to look ahead.

Sadly, no values had ever been built into Luis' life, and no encouragement had ever come his way. He had come to believe what, over the years, he had heard countless times: that yes, he was worthless, a river rat, a piraña. The world could only be a better place without him. Abandoned by his own mother, there could be no good in him.

Luis often looked ahead to his own death. The thought of it no longer frightened him. Somehow it actually fascinated him. He had grown so accustomed to his way of life that he couldn't really imagine any other. Every time he got the chance and a bit of stolen money in his pocket, he would board a boat for a new part of the world he knew best: Amazonía and its mighty Amazon River, bigger than Earth's next seven combined, with ten times the volume of the Mississippi, fifty times that of the Nile.

The river cast a spell over him and its magic held him fast. Farther and farther east he traveled. He loved the beautiful sunsets and always looked forward to the rising of the moon. Its silver rays cast a beam across the water. In his fleeting moments of pleasure, Luis imagined himself walking along it all the way to river's end and back again.

But Luis was certainly not prepared for the next stage in his journey. Two more giant bends in the mighty river, and there in front of him stood Iquitos, a city of three hundred thousand people, the place where the torments of his past would pale in comparison with what lay ahead.

He walked down the long plank of the Ticuna, and as if by premonition, shadows crossed his heart as dark clouds floated past his eyes. That rainy night he would meet a boy whom he unfortunately took to be a friend. In the following months, he was led into the depths of deprivation and into the deceitful world of drugs. Down, down, down. How much more could he take and how much lower must he go?

Months passed and he was consumed by disease, his face covered in tropical sores. Hungry and bloated, he soon had no energy to go on. He no longer stole. The police no longer noticed him. He was a mere shell and no one cared. He had spiraled to the very bottom. He finally collapsed.

On that day in 1993 when we found Luis, it had already been a difficult week at Scripture Union. None of us could stop thinking about Tico, a seven-year-old with a quick and ready smile who loved to laugh and listen to jokes. Tico had died unexpectedly of pneumonia just a few hours before Sergio, another of our boys, ran in crying, "Hermano Juan, Hermano Juan, there is a big boy in Belén dying in the garbage."

"Come, come with me," Juan Davila replied, as he jumped into one of our *motokars* (motorized rickshaws). "Tell me exactly where to go."

They drove to the corner of Hurtado and Calle Uno. They approached the large mound. The day was blistering hot and the garbage stank.

"We are glad someone came," said one of the market women, and another added, "We didn't really want to watch this boy die."

When Juan leaned over the frail body and started to lift it, he heard: "No me toques, quiero morir" (Don't touch me, I want to die). It was Luis Luna.

But Juan Dávila was not about to let him die. "Well, I don't want you to die, because I love you," he said, gently lifting the young man onto the rickshaw. A few minutes later, he and Sergio carried him to the floor that César had first slept on.

A few minutes later, Samuel came out of our director's office.

"Juan," he said, "why did you just lay this boy down on the floor? Can't you tell? He's dying."

He was soon lying on a simple bed in the large men's ward of Hospital Iquitos. Two long rows of beds lined the walls underneath the high windows. At the far end, for all to see, was the ever-present image of Jesus, dead on a cross.

A doctor came in. Juan and the boy who had found Luis stood by. After a very quick examination, the doctor looked at the frail body and said, "This boy's lungs are completely gone. He is in the very last stage of tuberculosis. He is dying and there is absolutely nothing I can do. I suggest you go buy four boards and take him away."

Luis heard this and now whispered, "Por favor, quiero vivir" (Please, I want to live).

"Doctor," said Juan, "I don't plan to nail up a coffin. This boy must live. May I make a deal with you? You as a man of science do your part, and I as a Christian will do mine."

The doctor, obviously intrigued by this proposition, agreed.

Juan and Sergio brought a pastor back to the hospital from a nearby church. The pastor talked to the dying boy. When the pastor had finished, Juan felt deeply confident that Luis not only had understood, but had given his life to the Master.

Juan and the boys all hurried away, first to the center and then to the homes of known Christians and to churches. "Pray for a boy who is dying in Hospital Iquitos. Ask God to heal him," was the simple request.

During the following week, Juan visited regularly and was thrilled to witness signs of improvement, ever so little at first but nevertheless encouraging. Luis listened attentively to Juan as he told him more and more about Jesus and the love he has for us. Luis, for once, felt included. This was a sign of the Spirit's work deep within him. He would learn in the hospital that when Jesus told us to take up our cross and follow him, he was not inviting us to a picnic. It would involve suffering and pain, but he would always be at our side. He would be the father, brother, and friend that Luis had never had. And he promised that at river's end was life evermore.

One morning when Juan arrived, he was excited to see Luis out of bed and walking, very slowly, from one sick man to the next. At each bed he would say: "Estoy vivo porque Jesús me sanó" (I am alive, because Jesus healed me).

One of the young men was Jaime, aged eighteen, who today drives one of our rickshaws. He had also been taken into the hospital from the street with tuberculosis. He came to faith in Christ through this simple testimony of Luis Luna.

Two weeks later, the hospital went on strike. Nurses, doctors, patients: everyone had to be out by two p.m. Juan went for Luis. As they were about to leave, the doctor came by, accompanied by several of his students.

"Señor Dávila," he said, "please tell me and my students what it is you did that made this boy live."

"Well," began Juan, "your professor and I made a deal. He as a man of science ..."

"I as a man of science did nothing," the doctor said. "Now, Señor Dávila, please tell us what you did."

Juan then spoke very simply of the power of Jesus to heal and of his great delight in answering the prayers of his children.

"Señor Dávila," the doctor said before leaving, "please come back someday to my hospital and tell me about this Jesus." Glancing at the crucifix high on the wall, he added, "He must be different from the one I have heard about."

Over the coming weeks, Luis grew by leaps and bounds into Christian maturity. His chains were broken. He flew higher and higher and came to love Jesus more and more. He was living proof of everything he now believed.

He looked at himself in the mirror. Malnutrition and disease had taken their toll. The smoldering fires of hurt and resentment would have flared up were it not for the fact that God had touched him. Luis knew that he was now in good hands and that his future would bring good things.

After two years, Luis approached Samuel in his office. "Hermano Samuel ..." he started off slowly. Then, gaining confidence, he said, "I must leave now, brother. The Big River is calling me."

"But ..." interrupted Samuel.

"I am well now," Luis said. "I feel strong and I know that God will go with me. I must now go back to my world and live my life there for Jesus. You have done so much for me. Now you must let me go."

"Go then, Luis, and tell others, or they'll never know."

A group of staff and boys gathered at the bank of the great, muddy river. Luis sat on the edge of his hammock strung across the upper deck. There were tears in many eyes that night as the boat pulled away and the kerosene lamps flickered in the distance.

The mountain pass
down which Zico
traveled to reach safety
— and salvation —
at Kimo, our retreat in
the jungle far below.

Brave Nancy Franco, director of Kimo. She faced down two terrorists with
the Word of God on her way to care for Christians in Satco, in the Andes
Mountains.

"Two Angels with Dirty Faces" — Nestor (left) and Tino.

Besides becoming the best of friends, Nestor and Tino make friends with many at our Girasoles Scripture Union Center in Lima and at Kimo.

Kimo is a tropical paradise where boys and girls from the jungle and the Andes Mountains encounter God through his word and his creation.

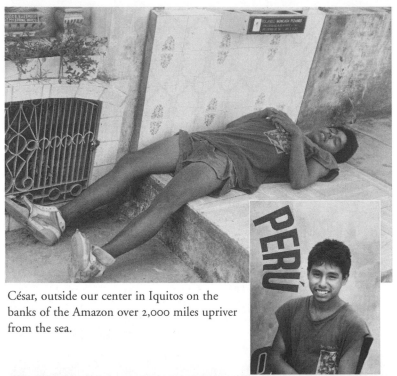

César, outside our center in Iquitos on the banks of the Amazon over 2,000 miles upriver from the sea.

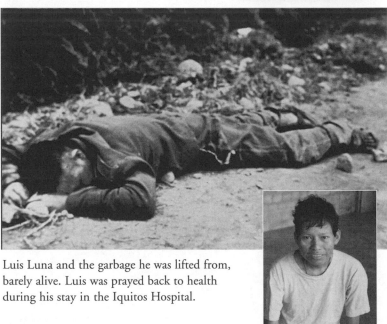

Luis Luna and the garbage he was lifted from, barely alive. Luis was prayed back to health during his stay in the Iquitos Hospital.

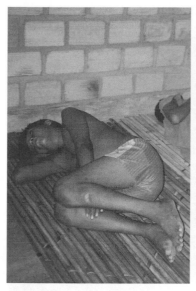

The boy who changed his name from Mayaco ("Rotten Fish") to Juan, at our center in Iquitos.

Little Tito came to our Puerto Alegria center off the street two years ago, when he was only four years old.

Often I am followed on my errands by boys in need of food. This group was waiting for me when I came out of a small hotel one afternoon. I was glad to meet their need with bread.

Poor areas from which our street boys come.

Love is a floor to sleep on, and that's all we had at this street boy home in Lima in the early days. Now we have bunk beds.

For boys who have never held a toy or eaten off a plate, it can be fun or just simply too much. Often, feeling unworthy, they go back to their lives on the street.

Here I am with some of our street boys, in Lima and at Kimo.

In the front row are our "Men of Valor" — actors in a play dramatizing their salvation and their desire to reach other boys with the gospel.

10

※

MAYACO
The Boy with Three Names

*T*iki climbed the tree in a flash and began to poke at an ant nest.

He should have known to keep his eyes on the ants instead of on the chihuaco bird. These birds are bright yellow and black and lay their eggs in a deep, beautifully woven straw pouch that hangs off the branches of the *palo chuncho*. They are believed to bring good luck, but that good luck certainly did nothing to stop the angered, stinging ants from swarming over Tiki's foot and leg.

Down below, his mother reclined in her hammock as she stirred the boiling pot on the fire. Her older boys were out hunting the choro monkey. If they found none, they would go fishing. One way or another they always managed to come home with something. They were good boys and she was proud of them all. Her peace and quiet came to an end when she heard her little one screaming.

"What have you done now?" she asked as her young son ran up to her in a panic. "Ya ves, ya ves" (You see, you see), she scolded as she brushed off the last of the stinging *isula*. He'd been forbidden to poke at the nests. She rubbed the healing sap of a thick vine on the bites and said, "Now get into that hammock over there and think about what you did."

Ants or no ants, those early days were great fun. No end of yuca could be had from the clearing just next to theirs. Everything was everyone's and no one went hungry: not only was there yuca, but also fish, bananas, and every now and then a choro monkey. There is no private ownership of property along the limitless banks of jungle rivers, and were it not for the frequent spearings, life on the edges of the far-flung tribe would be unbeatable. At least, that is, in the part of the world you can touch. Underneath and above is a different story: that is where the demons and the spirits hold sway.

Little Tiki would grow up to have no memories of his father and very few of his mother. What would remain vivid in his mind were the sounds and stories of the jungle, and above all, the *brujo* (witch doctor).

Tiki had been in his hammock long enough. "It doesn't sting any more," he told his mother. "I promise I'll never go up the palo chuncho again. May I go look for my brothers? Maybe they'll need my help bringing back all the monkey meat."

The woman covered her mouth and laughed. "You are so funny, my little Tiki. You sing, you whistle, you jump, and you dance. Just like your mother used to. Now run along."

Excitement awaited Tiki down at water's edge. The boys had accidentally landed a six-foot-long *puraque* (electric eel). "Wow, what a big one!" shouted Tiki as he ran, jumping over fallen balsa logs. "Do you eat those?"

"Yes, Tikito," they laughed. "You may start right now," said the older boy, as he poked at the still-squirming creature. They knew an eel this size could easily paralyze one of the bigger boys and do considerably more to someone as small as Tiki — in the water, that is. This one was now high and dry and totally harmless. Soon it would be dead.

They got two big sticks and a little one for Tiki and lifted the eel into their dugout canoe. They paddled down the long sweep of river before them and then around the first meander. Downstream was always easier and soon they were unloading their trophy at the clearing of their best friend, Miope.

But there was to be no fun and laughter in Miope's clearing that day. The boys didn't understand what was going on, but they knew something was up. They threw the dead eel back into the river and asked Miope what was happening. He didn't answer because he didn't really know. Tiki's friends thought it was best to get right back home. The older boy got into the canoe and started rowing upstream by himself. There was no point in overloading the canoe when the other two could take the trail.

On the way, Tiki stopped for a moment to play beneath the achiote tree. "Slow down," he called after his brother. "I want to get some achiote seeds to paint my face." The dark, waxy-red seeds were used in the tribe by dancers, warriors, and, of course, the brujos.

Tiki pulled down a whole stem of dried-up pods. He broke one open and soon he was looking like a miniature killer. "Attack!" he cried, setting off down the trail in pursuit of his imaginary enemy.

It's strange how parents around the world encourage their little boys to play at killing one another by buying them toy weapons — or, as in the case of Tiki's mother, laughing when her painted little man climbed up onto the tarima bark platform of her jungle dwelling. But this time little Tiki wasn't laughing — he had a terrified look on his face.

"Mother, help me wash this off," the little boy said, brushing back

big tears. "I'm afraid, Mother. What's going to happen? I saw the
brujo on the trail leading to Miope's clearing. They were waiting for
him." Then he broke out crying. "Brujo looked right at me. My face
was painted. He said something, but I didn't hear." Then with a big
sob, he said, "I'm afraid."

Tiki's mother didn't know what to say.

That night passed very slowly for Tiki. The forest is not silent at
night. It bursts into life. Frogs croak. There is the unmistakable noise
of the chicharra and the excited chatter of a variety of night monkeys
— all in different keys, yet somehow blending beautifully together.
But not this night, at least not for Tiki, whose sleep was riddled
with bad dreams. What does a child do when he awakens from a
nightmare only to discover that what he's looking at is worse?

Tiki looked out from his hammock and saw the witch doctor with
all the men from this clearing sitting around the open fire. What
were they talking about? What might they be planning to do? Tiki's
imagination went wild as he curled up tight in his hammock like a
frightened puppy. Though very young, he had heard stories of
children thrown into the forest for the animals to eat, or choked with
vines or buried alive.

Tiki soon saw lightning strike and heard loud thunder. He feared
that the chaos in the heavens would awaken every evil spirit deep
within the earth. Then, finally, he fell back to sleep.

The dawn came clear and warm over the silent river. Smoke rose
through the thatch of every hut in the clearing as fires were lit for the
first yuca of the day. For Tiki it was fish, as well. He was busily
picking the bones out of the fish when Miope came over to play.

Everything seemed back to normal, almost too good to be true —
that is, until his mother took her boy aside.

"You must not cry now when I tell you what the witch doctor is going to do," she told him. Before he could say anything, this loving mother held her boy tightly and continued: "He is not going to kill you. He is just going to take your teeth away. He wouldn't tell me what happened in the next clearing, but he did say that he saw you on the trail yesterday — the boy with the achiote, he said."

"How will he take my teeth away?" asked Tiki.

"He didn't say. But he won't pull them out. He said it wouldn't hurt. So don't worry, Tikito, Mother will mash your yuca very soft and take all the bones out of your fish. You can suck on the soft parts of the monkey. Use your tongue, too."

What happened then was to continue until Tiki was about ten. The brujo came back time and time again to rub his upper teeth with the hard root of a jungle vine. It felt like a soft wooden brush. Tiki's teeth receded and eventually they were gone. The evil spirit identified by the witch doctor had been appeased.

During those same years, this boy's eyes were to see more of the horrors of jungle life than could be wished on anyone: killings, stealing of women and children, and the never-ending murmuring and mysterious presence of the witch doctor.

What happened on that day when he last saw his mother and was taken away on the big boat, he will never know. As the vessel made the big bend downriver, Tiki saw his brothers on the sandbank far away, and Miope on his sandbank a bit closer. No one waved. No one had said goodbye. Maybe they, too, didn't know what was happening. Maybe they, too, never would.

The man in charge of Tiki never talked. He spent most of the day just sitting on the rim of his hammock looking out over the water. So did Tiki. One river flowed into another and that one into the next, until Tiki lost count. He kept an anxious eye on the sun, now on one side, then the other, sometimes behind, and occasionally straight ahead, as the rivers squirmed around the forest, carrying the boat farther and farther from home and ever closer to the "civilized world" that would mistreat and abuse him and eventually discard him as trash.

A few days and nights later, Tiki did not remember how many, they arrived in Iquitos. He had never seen a house or a building, a street or a light post. He had seen many boats and canoes, but never a car, truck, or bus. He and the man took a ride in a rickshaw down to Puerto Belén, where the man, still a stranger, "lost" him. From then on, and for the next four years, everything would be downhill for this boy.

Over time, he met other abandoned street boys. Each had his own story to tell, his own problems. "¿A quién le interesa tu vida?" (Who's interested in your life?) an older boy snapped at Tiki one day.

When Tiki didn't answer, the older boy continued to mock him. "¿Tu nombre?" (What's your name?).

Tiki remained silent out of confusion and fear.

"Mayaco, seguro" (Probably Mayaco), one of the boys jeered, and they all laughed. The new name stuck.

On perhaps the only good day he would remember of his years in the streets, he met a friend. "What's your name?" he asked the boy.

"Pitin. ¿Y el tuyo?"

"Mayaco."

That was simple enough, and it marked the beginning of a friendship that would be strengthened as it was molded in the fire. They were to become inseparable. They would run together, steal together, hide together. And sink ever deeper into sin and depravation together. By the time they were fourteen, what had they not done, what had not been done to them? They were the throwaway children of Iquitos, the ones even the police grow tired of whipping.

—⁂—

One day in 1990, Juan Dávila walked past the police station on Calle Morona. He saw a street boy sitting on the far side. He sat on the sidewalk beside him.

"¿Tienes hambre?" (Are you hungry?) he asked.

"No," said the boy, staring straight ahead at the big entrance gate.

Juan knew better. The boy looked starved. "Sí, tienes hambre" (Yes, you are hungry).

"What's your name?"

"Mayaco."

"Mayaco, let me go and bring you something to eat."

"But I won't eat it until I eat it with Pitin."

"Who's Pitin?"

"Pitin has been in there over two days now," he said, pointing to the high prison wall. "I won't move from here until he comes out. And I won't eat until he comes out."

Juan returned the next day just in time. Mayaco was still sitting there when the gate opened and a gaunt, yellow-skinned boy with sunken eyes was shoved out.

"You are Pitin, and I am Hermano Juan (Brother John). I was once a street boy also. In Lima. Jesus rescued me. He and I are friends to boys like you. He got beaten by the police, too."

The three walked to the Belén market and ate a plate of rice and turtle eggs.

From that day on, it was no longer Mayaco and Pitin, it was Mayaco and Pitin and Hermano Juan. Juan became their friend, their protector, their hero. When he would go home at night, they would often fall into their old ways, but Hermano Juan would always forgive them. But the thing he most wanted for them, they would not listen to.

"God is dead," they would say. "We want to live. He's in that big church, dead on a cross."

All Juan could do was pray that they would some day come to an encounter with the living Christ. He talked to them about Scripture Union and the center for boys like them. But they were fearful. They had walked into too many traps before. This would be just another, they thought.

Or would it? One day Pitin braved it. He had a meal, listened to a Bible story, and watched. There were no signs of foul play. Furthermore, he saw some boys he recognized from the street. He thanked Juan and left. Two days later and he was back, still without Mayaco. By then, Pitin had met Samuel, Noemi, and also Rosita, the cook. She had a beautiful, quiet way about her. He loved her food and cheerful manner. In fact, they all seemed *buena gente* (good people).

The next time, when Mayaco came along with Pitin, it was a big day for Hermano Juan. He had brought them both to shelter. He knew that the rest was up to God.

The first time I met Mayaco, he already seemed fairly well integrated into the group. He slept on the upper porch floor along with César, Luis Luna, and the rest, and eagerly devoured all the food he could lay his hands on, as well as all the Bible stories he could hear. Especially the ones about Jesus, Hermano Juan's friend. Of all the people in the stories, Jesus was definitely the one who fit in best with the life of a street boy, who would feel most at home in Puerto Belén, forgotten and rejected.

I had two questions for Samuel. The first was, "This boy's bottom teeth are beautiful, the top ones are gone. Do you know anything about it?" The second was, "Juan says that this boy is responsible for the holes in the brick wall upstairs. Is it true — that he has been eating the wall?"

"As for his teeth," said Samuel, "we know nothing from Mayaco except that when he was a child, a witch doctor shaved them away and that he has no idea of his age or where he came from, except that it was some distant river. As for the bricks, it is true. He does eat brick. He says it tastes better than dirt. A doctor told me that a starving body often craves minerals present in the dirt."

As time went on, I became friendly with this charming boy. "What would you like to do when you are a grown man?" I once asked him. His immediate answer was, "I would like to be like Hermano Juan."

⌒

Months went by. When I returned to Iquitos for the next of my regular visits, Noemi and Samuel had big news for me.

"Actually, it's great news," Samuel told me when I reached his office. "Sit down and let me tell you."

He shifted the tabletop fan toward the straight wooden chair he knew I'd sit in.

I unbuttoned my shirt and sat down. "Tell me," I said.

"Well, you know what it's been like with Mayaco, right? Since your last visit, things changed and it seemed as though every mention of God was being turned into a giant step backward. We were beginning to think that the truth would never sink in. He never gave us so much as one ray of hope as he had earlier on. Quite frankly, it had become quite discouraging. I remember he was always one of your favorites, but could never imagine quite why."

"It started with that wall incident," I interrupted. "You know, the wall he was eating from."

A big smile broke right across Samuel's handsome face. "Well, two days ago he gave us the surprise," he said.

I held my breath. Could it be?

"Mayaco accepted Christ. He prayed, asking God to forgive all his sins: the ones in the forest, but especially all the ones here on the streets and the marketplace and Belén. He asked him to wash him clean and give him a new start. When he finished this long prayer, he looked up and gave this big, beautiful ..."

"Toothless ..."

"Yes, beautiful, toothless smile. Then, looking my way, he said very deliberately, as though underlining each word, 'Ya no soy Mayaco, mi nombre es Juan'" (I no longer am Mayaco, my name is John).

"Samuel, what does Mayaco mean?"

"In street language," he said, "Mayaco means rotten fish."

"And why Juan?" I asked, as if I didn't know.

"Juan Dávila, remember?"

I went down the steps looking for this boy. I saw him coming with his big — yes, toothless — smile. His incredible life story flashed through my mind. I called out to him, "Juan!" There were tears in my eyes as I gave him an extra big *abrazo*.

11

TARIRI
Ruler of the Seven Rivers

Consumed by passionate hate for their enemies and propelled by a sense of their own destiny, they spear, kill, cut off heads, and torch the houses of their victims. Tariri had more shrunken heads around his waist than any other and was the undisputed chief of the Shapra tribe.

Yet, in answer to much prayer and the courage of two brave missionaries, Tariri — the fabled killer of killers — would become the man who prays to Jesus before he goes out hunting for food.

Let me tell you a bit about this amazing man. Much of what follows is in his own words, spoken to Wycliffe Bible Translator friends of mine, Lorrie Anderson and John Tuggy, in preparation for the book *Tariri, My Story*.

"My Grandfather Totarika was a terrible killer," said Tariri. "He killed and killed. My father, Nochumata, went killing with his father. He followed his father and was taught by him. Old Maama and

Korima also taught my father how to kill. They each had their own hard palm-wood spear when they went out to kill.

"There were many, many Candoshi away back then. Now they are almost all gone. They ran away. All the big chiefs and the older ones were killed and only the young men were left over. The people ran away so they would not be killed by their enemies. My father was the chief of the Shapra people of the Candoshi. Each one lived in his own place and had his own people.

"The Achuales also killed many of our people with spears. My father was very great and very strong. How many people he killed! He went killing with his friend Chumpi. They killed Huambisas and Achuales. My father would gather together many men from the Chapuri and Chuinta rivers. They did whatever he ordered. They killed many Achuales on the Mawuia River.

"Our ancestors taught us, 'If people come to your house to make an attack, do not be afraid. You just chase them back into the woods and kill them. If you do not, they will kill you.'"

Tariri's words and my life in the jungles of Peru brought many questions to my mind. How different are the Shapras, the Ashaninka, the Aucas to our own culture? "Kill them before they kill us, and preferably somewhere other than our land" sounded troublingly familiar. My own people also go through training in preparation and then honor those who have been successful on the field.

"When boys are about ten years of age," said Tariri, "they are told, 'Spend time with the *koraka* (the chief). Spend time with the *korakas* (the people who kill).' You have to go for a long time with the *korakas* to learn how it is done. One who kills someone and takes his head and shrinks it becomes a chief. Our ancestors learned and taught us. It was a man who killed and took many heads who became greater than all other people. He became a great chief.

"My uncle Kasimoro and his friend named Mbisa taught me, and I went out to kill. They even taught me how to take heads. You only go after someone who is empty handed, somebody who is just sitting there, just kind of dreaming. You can dash at him and spear him. That way you are able to kill quickly. That is easy. Our people kill when it is almost wanting to get dark.

"They took the women for wives. My father had six wives. The men loved their wives, but the women fought with each other. They would say, 'What do you want to be with her for? Why do you neglect me?' Each wife wanted his attention. I only had two. I wanted to kill in order to take many women. Then I would have many wives and raise many children. We would be one big happy family, I thought. One woman has one child and then, much later, many moons later, another? That is no good."

Tucked away in the remote and uncharted headwaters of the Amazon in a particularly dense part of the jungle, Tariri and his Shapra tribal group had only the sketchiest notion of life beyond the borders of their own forested kingdom. The vague image of outsiders that was projected into this obscure corner was at best a veiled threat to their security.

The gospel was first brought to the Pushaga River in the 1960s by Lorrie Anderson and her friend Doris Cox. They were joined later by John and Sheila Tuggy and Rachel Saint, whose brother Nate was one of the five missionaries martyred in the early 1950s by the neighboring Aucas. They and the Candoshi, of which Tariri's Shapras are a part, have much in common, including fear and hate of the Viracocha.

"I hated the white man," said Tariri. "I stood ready to kill any who might come to my domain. I was Ruler of the Seven Rivers."

Only the direct intervention of God can explain what happened next. A small airplane landed and then took off from a jungle river, leaving behind two Viracochas on a narrow, shady riverbank smack in the middle of Chief Tariri's Shapra land. Lorrie and Doris were brought before the warrior himself. The obvious did not happen. Instead, Tariri gave them the safest status of all, that of daughters. He named them Monchanki and Mpawachi.

"Mpawachi talked much with me," said Tariri. "She taught me what God said. She said killing was bad. Hating, too. God will punish us very much. He will put those who kill into darkness."

Over the following months, the missionaries learned enough of the language to be able to present the simple yet powerful message of God.

"I wondered about Jesus," Tariri said later. "What shall I do? What shall I do? Shall I leave killing? Shall I stop fighting? If I leave fighting, people will think I am not a chief anymore. I will make myself greater than all other chiefs. I should have killed everyone. This is how I thought, not knowing what to do. Then I thought, 'What am I saying?' After a while I thought, 'That is what I will do. I will love God.'

"I had already decided in my heart about God, but I was not thinking about it as I came home from hunting, running along in my ragged skirt with my dart holder over my shoulders. I was thinking about the food I had caught.

"Mpawachi called, 'Come here. Come quickly.' I was ashamed. There was dirt all over me, and there was monkey blood on my back where I had carried the spider monkey after shooting him with my blowgun. Mpawachi said, 'When are you going to receive Jesus? Receive him right now.'

"I said, 'All right.' My heart was so happy when I said it. I received Jesus with my ragged skirt on, without ever having had a bath. Then we talked with God. When I talked with Jesus, I said, 'You clean me with your blood. Put good in my heart. My heart is dirty. Throw all the dirt away. I will follow only you. Take out everything that holds me back. Throw it far away. Send it away.' When I said that, Jesus came into my heart."

Many times in the coming years, Tariri had been tempted to take revenge — for example, when he was sold a faulty outboard motor. "For a bad dugout outboard motor, I used to take heads," he told the man who had cheated him. "But because Jesus overcame me, I forgive you."

He learned to obey God and love his enemies and those who spitefully used him. He ordered his tribe to no longer kill, even if they were attacked. God honors those who honor him. Tariri and the many Christians in his tribe are living witnesses to this truth.

The upriver nation tribe is an example. "I had been angry and thought, 'I want to kill all the upriver people,'" Tariri said. "But God said no, so because I was kept from doing it, they still live. God won."

"'It is because Tariri loves God that he does not come to kill us,' they say. 'God changed him.' That news gets around about me now."

And so it has.

⁓

I had a growing desire to meet this man and set out to do so with a group my wife, Marty, and I put together: twenty-one adventurous teenage boys.

We set off from Kimo on a ten-day trek through the jungle very early one rainy morning.

I had never seen so many monkeys in my life, nor have I since. They were hanging off the branches of a tree at the end of the Aguaytia Bridge like mangos in the month of December.

I had always wondered what this place would be like, because it was here that my Aunt Viola had found my friend Jimmy. Whether he had ever been given another name, I do not know. He was always Jimmy to me. The Aguaytia is the domain of the Cashibos. When a mother dies, the baby is thrown into this big river. But Jimmy was rescued and grew up happy in the nearby mission home, so I was personally overjoyed to have been able to come this way.

The mission home is not far from the place where quinine was accidentally discovered, before the arrival of the Spaniards, by a dying Indian. This led to millions of people around the world being saved from death by malaria.

Things started heating up. These were the days before Shining Path, which began its activities in the 1980s. Terrorism had never crossed our minds, save for the sporadic reports we read about in the newspapers regarding Elías Cano, who frightened people out of their wits when he staged surprise attacks with his small band of outlaws. I believed all this to be happening only in the far south of Peru.

Darkness overtook us before we found a place to sleep. We never expected comfort on this trip, or we never would have come, but I felt it was our responsibility to keep the group as safe from danger as was reasonable in these remote parts. So we cleared away the debris and cobwebs, checked for snakes, and then settled down for the night in an abandoned concrete room. The building had previously served the Peruvian Air Force at the end of a jungle runway as a frontier defense post in its surveillance of neighboring Colombia.

We moved on early the next morning and found out later, through an army intelligence report, that, after we left, our overnight lodge had served as a hiding place for none other than Elías Cano and his men. They were themselves seeking more permanent refuge in the forest. Running accidentally into someone you fear in Amazonia is about as likely as one needle finding another on a golf course. But we were safe.

The next portion of our trip was one of incredible beauty. How liberating it was to see a massive cliff shrouded in dense vegetation and know that we were not looking at Mankoite, the demon of the Mountain's Face; to stand at the entrance of a cave and know that it was not the Mouth of Katsivoveri; to feel the rain and see lightning and know that God was not angry. How rewarding to come to the end of a long day, eat tuna fish and bananas for supper, and sit around a crackling campfire knowing that all was well. It certainly made for a good rest, in spite of the often unexplained sounds in the night.

The next big event was the two-day trip we needed to make down the Huallaga Valley. My own little boy, Johnny, said to me once when I was obviously lost: "Daddy, don't worry. If there is no path, we'll make one." I have often thought of that. I would be more likely to follow that advice when alone with him than when responsible for over twenty kids, I decided to avoid the shortcuts that the trails afford in favor of the longer, meandering river.

Early the first morning, as the first rays of light broke the cloudless sky, we gathered at the riverbank around our large raft made of twenty balsa tree trunks, broke a bottle of Inca Kola against her "hull," and amid cheers christened her Tariri II.

We had just come too close for comfort to a large, deadly poisonous *shushupe* (bushmaster), and so everyone scrambled quickly aboard. The *balsero* (ferryman) whom we had paid to guide us was in charge of navigation. Marty was in charge of the 250 oranges and ever-present tuna fish, and I assumed my task as troubleshooter-at-large.

Our raft was bound tight with liana vines and strong tree bark and measured 24 feet by 16. It had a raised platform in the middle and was covered by a banana-leaf roof. Brightly colored birds darted in front of us or dipped across the water in their happy flight. What more could we ask for? Swimming was great from both sides, and safe:

piraña bite and swarm only when blood is present, and among the lot of us, we had nothing more to show than mosquito bites.

The raft pulled over to the side at dusk because the balsero needed to sleep. None of us relished the idea of getting stuck on a sandbank with nothing but turtle eggs until the next rainy season, but what a night it was! The gentle breeze turned to a howling wind. It whipped through the clearing and lashed at the tops of trees and at the thatch of the only hut within sight. We grabbed our few possessions and ran for cover. Fortunately for us, the hut had been abandoned. Huddled together, we all somehow managed to fit. Everyone had conveniently forgotten to bring the tuna fish, which was just fine. There would be more for the next day and skipping a meal on this trip was actually a pleasure.

The locals called the place Sharinkaveri, the stronghold of demons. Kamari, as they call them, are legion and consider all humans their legitimate prey. Their insatiable urge is to inflict damage on people and make their lives miserable, which must have been the case with the family that abandoned this house. Or someone may have died in it, in which case everyone else would have quickly left, assuming the new *Kamari* to have a preference for his old home.

But none of this worried us. Happy to be under a roof, we all promptly fell asleep. But not for long.

Someone broke the silence. "¿Escuchaste?" (Did you hear?)

"¿Qué?"

"Escucha, escucha" (Listen, listen).

One by one we all woke up. If we hadn't heard at first, we certainly did now: the distant roar of the otorongo. These cats weigh up to 190 pounds. The sound was very distant at first, but slowly became louder, and now was unmistakable. The low muffled deep roar sent ripples up and down the flesh of even the bravest of us. Then, fortunately, we remembered who we were and who had promised to be with us. The panther's roar slowly became more and more distant.

Still, morning could not come soon enough, and we were all up and away in record time. As we climbed aboard our raft, we saw two men down at riverside beating out barbasco root. The tips of arrows would be dipped into this most potent of poisons. Maybe they, too, had heard last night's prowler.

That second day on the river started off as relaxing and great fun for all, except for Marty and me. We knew that the trickiest part of the trip would come mid-afternoon when the balsero's skill would be put to the test big time. Things would not be made any easier by a load of excitable and nervous teenagers. Ignorance is bliss. We deliberately kept them in the dark about the careful maneuvering our captain would have to make.

Beyond a tight, hairpin turn, the large yet smaller Mayo River flows into the Huallaga from the left, creating an immense and very dangerous whirlpool, known to suck down bigger vessels than ours. Just beyond this, the mighty Huallaga plunges over the Vaquero Malpaso Falls. Tightly snuggled between the two, on the left bank unfortunately, was the tiny village of Shapaja. Our raft needed to barely touch the far right sweep of the counterclockwise whirlpool in order to get past this first hurdle. Then it needed to get over to the village before being taken over the falls. Quite impossible without help. So Shapaja had a large dugout with an outboard motor at the ready, to pull in the rafts on their way to Vaquero.

When the time came, we pointed out the Mayo River to the boys and told them to get ready to disembark. Everything went perfectly. We were met in Shapaja by Marguerite Hale, a missionary who knew of our travels. She had spent many hours watching out for us to ensure that the canoe with the motor was ready to tow the raft in. She had herself survived the falls strapped to a balsa tree trunk years before and didn't want to see us go over. (A twenty-log balsa will take twenty people. All will be strapped to a log. If the balsa breaks up, each log will eventually float to a side of the river.) That night we thanked the Lord for Marguerite when she told us that she had to pay the owner of the canoe to come out for us. He had decided to "let them go over," believing the raft to belong to a rival he had no interest in sparing.

Our travels continued and eventually led us to our final destination, Yarinacocha. Here we would meet Tariri himself. Expectations were high. It was not every day that one meets such a legendary figure — a headhunter — and, especially, incredible as it may seem, one who now loved his enemies.

I knew Tariri was on Wycliffe's base, but I could not think of a way to meet him. In one of my unwise moments, I came up with a crazy idea: we could stage an attack, with Tariri himself as the main actor. That afternoon's close encounter in Lake Yarina with an anaconda, combined with the very basic sleeping quarters we had been given on the very edge of the forest on a moonless night, provided the ideal background to my foolish plan. It would not be difficult for me to work the boys up to a pitch. After all, by now tension was already high.

I asked my missionary friend Phil Cheeseman for help. He lived on the base and knew the people closest to Tariri. My plan went like this. A few minutes before Tariri's arrival at our hut, Phil would come by to remind us to be very quiet at night, lest we arouse the anger of the nearby Indians. After that, we'd all be in utter silence, desperately trying to fall asleep. Then, at a signal from Phil, I would shine my bright light on the door. Standing there in the doorway would be

Tariri, spear in hand. Wow, what a plan! Phil went along with every detail. He got to the chief through an interpreter.

I was all set for the "attack" when Phil came by with news for me. "Sorry, my friend. Tariri was not amused."

"What did he say?" I asked, with childish disappointment.

"He said, 'I do not understand. Why do you ask this of me? I do not kill. I used to. I took many heads. I now love Jesus. I do not pretend to kill either. That is very bad. Why are you here? Why do you want this?'"

The boys never knew of my surprise. Just as well.

Tariri was right. In fact, very much so. I fell asleep that night thinking of stores, the world over, full of toy guns for our little boys to play with, pretending to kill each other. Oh God, when will we ever learn?

So, we met Tariri on his ground, doing what he now knows how to do best. A large number of us gathered in a big hall to hear this amazing man talk. A hush fell over the audience as the King of the Seven Rivers walked in. He spoke of the King of Kings who had "taken" his heart and was busily preparing a place for him on his river.

We will not soon forget this man, the long journey that brought us to him, and the lesson he taught us.

12

API
An Unfinished Story

*T*he campfire was low, made the beautiful way Ashaninka Indians know how to make it. The flames dimly lit up the faces of the people around. Everyone was there, even Aunt Sharani and Uncle.

Api, who was usually asleep by this time of night, was wide awake as Grandfather told his story.

"Let me tell you about bats," he began slowly. He hunched up over the fire as everyone became absolutely silent.

"Long ago the bat was a person. He was a wicked man who married a sweet and quiet girl. He bit her hands and arms endlessly. She became very weak and sick. This sickness made her skin turn yellow. So she prepared a gourd full of *masato* drink which she herself had made by chewing the yuca root and spitting it into a bowl to ferment. Her husband drank it. She gave him another, then another. He drank all night. Then he fell down with a thud and was asleep. To keep warm he drew himself up into his cushma. While he was sleeping, the young wife sewed up the cushma, foot holes, arm holes, head hole, and all.

"Then some canaries came along. One of them felt very sorry for the man and said, 'Let us join him in the cushma. We want to drink masato with him.' So the girl opened the cushma and let the canaries in. Then she sewed it up again.

"When the man started to wake up, the wife dumped water on him. No matter how hard he fought to get out, he couldn't. He thrashed and thrashed inside the cushma. Then suddenly many bats came out. He had turned into bats! They escaped and took refuge in the cliffs. That is where they live.

"When people die," Grandfather continued, "many of them become bats. They, too, live in cliffs above the river near the whirlpools. They fly at night and suck people's blood. They live in the cliffs with the evil spirits that claim the souls of children. These spirits are almost as bad as Viracocha."

Little Api jumped up. "Please tell me who the Viracocha is!"

Grandfather raised his voice as though it was harder for a small one to understand. "Well, my little one, in the lower levels of the earth where the spirits live, the great serpent Nonki dominates. His reflection is the rainbow."

Api's eyes looked as if they were going to jump clean out of her head. She loved rainbows.

"Yes, my little one, when you see the rainbow, it is Nonki's reflection you are seeing. The jungle lake is the gateway to the great underworld. Alligators that live in the lake are evil spirits, too. It is from this lake that one night Viracocha appeared. He is like a man, except that he is tall and often pink and always has short hair. It is not long and pretty like ours. It is as though a bat had chewed on it. Hair also grows on his face. Well, Viracocha got on a raft and went to the river's end, from where he comes back every now and then to bring harm. His soul comes from the stomach of a demon."

Grandfather didn't seem to want to pursue this subject any further. "I will finish by telling you about the white-throated sparrow, and then we must all go to sleep."

He drew himself yet closer to the fire. "When swallows with white throats circle around in the sky, they are waiting to take the spirit of someone who at that moment is dying. They will hold his spirit until darkness falls. It will then begin to rain. The wind will blow. The choro monkey's howl will pierce the silence. A streak of jagged light will be seen splintering the sky. This is the spirit being hurled to the ground and transformed immediately into a demon. His transformation will be signaled by a loud, cracking sound. Sometimes even the mighty capirona tree will be split from top to bottom as a dread reminder of the fate of all humans. The mighty jungle at night is the unchallenged domain of evil. That is why we sit by the campfire. We don't wander around at night."

⌒

The next morning, Keesha was watching her little girl as she played. "Come here, child," she scolded. "I don't want you ever again out of my sight. Is that clear?"

"Yes, yes, Mother," answered little Api as she pounced on an unsuspecting green lizard.

"Some wonder I'm nervous," continued the woman, "after that awful story Grandfather chose to tell last night."

Just then the little Ashaninka Indian girl saw a big yellow and orange butterfly bounce by. She didn't know whether to let go of the lizard, which she now held in one hand, or the giant cricket, which she held in the other.

"Leave those horrid little insects alone," Keesha said with a frown that suppressed a smile. She adored her little girl. Other than this beautiful child, Keesha and Teni had very little. They each wore a handwoven, gown-like cushma, with three strings of brightly colored beads for her and a parrot feather bracelet for him. Then there were two clay cooking pots and two hammocks in their jungle dwel-ling. The hut itself consisted of a *tarima* (raised floor) and four poles supporting a high, palm-thatched roof.

"Keesha, Keesha," called Teni. "Come quickly. Aunt Sharani needs you now!"

Keesha glanced back in the direction of her daughter as she started up the slippery clay path. "I'll be back soon, my little hummingbird," she called. It was only a matter of minutes before she would be beside Aunt Sharani.

The air was filled with jungle sounds. Sounds of birds, of insects, the distant call of the Maqui monkey and the buzzing of bees. Twice Keesha slipped, twice she fell. Each time she laughed as she got back on her feet and carried on toward the clearing. Ashaninka women always laugh when they fall. Everyone laughs, even the children. They never laugh, though, when a man falls. Men are strong and wise and steady.

"Teni, you called me. What is the matter?"

"I called you three times, you foolish woman."

"But I only heard once and came running," she protested.

"How many times did you fall?"

"Only once," she lied.

He laughed. She laughed, too. Teni and Keesha had loved each other since they were both very young. They still did. They enjoyed life. Laughing was part of it. But this was no time to laugh.

"Now you must do something about Aunt Sharani," Teni urged.

"Quick, quick, do something."

Aunt Sharani lay on the tarima, looking straight up at the thatched roof. Her face was hot, her eyes distant. Her breathing was not good: sometimes fast, then suddenly slow.

"Call ..." they could barely hear her say. Then her voice was gone.

Teni leaned over his old aunt and tried to hear. "Say it again," he insisted again and again.

Then finally they heard, "Call ... the ... Brujo."

"Of course, Aunt Sharani," Teni fairly shouted, as he jumped off the tarima onto the ground and darted down the muddy path toward the stream, then the river, then the jungle trail through earth's densest rainforest. He ran for at least as long as it takes to build a fire and make water boil. He then followed the big river, sometimes walking, sometimes swimming. After crossing it three times he reached Boca Tigre (the Tiger's Mouth). He would be bringing back the Brujo.

In the meantime, Keesha sat beside Aunt Sharani, fanning her with a huge balsa leaf and cooling her forehead with water. Soon Uncle would be back from hunting and he would gladly look after his wife.

"Ah, my little girl," said Keesha as little Api came running into the clearing, the huge blue butterfly and cricket now mashed between her fingers.

"My lizard escaped and I slipped and fell in the stream seven times," Api said.

They both laughed. Api climbed up on the tarima beside her mother and old Aunt Sharani, who was asleep now. Api curled up and soon was fast asleep, too.

Keesha looked out over her little world. It was a good one. It must stay good for a long time, she thought, as she studied the small group of dwellings. The little clearing had but five huts around it, yet it was large for an Ashaninka village. Her dark brown face opened up into a big smile. Her long silky black hair hung almost to the tarima as she sat cross-legged beside Aunt Sharani. Her big eyes brightened. Keesha was beautiful and young. "My house is the best," she thought. "My family is the best."

Aunt Sharani stirred. A look of pain passed over her face. Keesha touched her forehead. Her fever wasn't going away.

Before long, Uncle returned to Aunt Sharani's side. Keesha explained her condition to him, then picked up her little Api and carried her back to their own hut.

Just thinking about Grandfather's stories had upset Keesha, especially because in recent days she had seen more white-throated sparrows than usual. "That is why I must always keep a close watch on my little girl," she thought.

⌒◞

There would be no campfire that night, for the session with the Brujo would go long into the night. As she walked, barefoot, back to Aunt Sharani's hut, Keesha held her cushma tightly to herself. She sat beside Teni, her legs hanging loosely from the tarima floor. The Brujo was already preparing to begin his ritual.

She could scarcely believe what she was seeing: the witch doctor was going to blow smoke on Aunt Sharani, something that was done only in very serious cases. Keesha had seen it done once before, when Teni's older brother had died.

Keesha clung close to Teni's side. He was strong and he was kind to her. He was her man, and she needed his protection and strength now more than ever. She dreaded having to witness the witch doctor at work, but she had no choice. Every adult in the village had to be present.

As night fell, the jungle came alive. The rasping noise of the chicharra, the chirping of the crickets, that indescribable combination of sounds made by the many owls, night monkeys, and a hundred and one bugs and insects. Everyone sat in absolute silence exchanging glances. No one said a word, not even the men, not even Grandfather. Everyone was in total awe of the Brujo. A sea of faces, intent and expressionless, was painted against a background of thatch and darkness.

The moon had been out earlier, but now clouds were once again covering it over. There was no light except for a little candle that burned dimly between poor old Aunt Sharani and the Brujo. The witch doctor busied himself working on the tobacco paste that he would rub on the old lady's chest. Then he sat back against one of the four poles of the hut and began to quietly smoke Ayahuasca. This is a most potent hallucinatory drug, many times stronger than the coca leaf, which grows in abundance in the jungle. Within the length of time it would take him to get to the stream and back, he would be in a trance. This was necessary to bring about a cure or to divine the culprit causing the illness. All illness is seen by the Indians to be caused by Kamari, an evil spirit, often through a small child, a girl. It is believed that crickets teach small children witchcraft.

The Brujo, without a doubt, would know what to do.

The villagers watched and waited. The Brujo was now very clearly in a trance. He asked for an earthen vessel of steaming water to be brought. Anticipating this, the oldest woman had built a fire over a circle of stones and had everything ready. The boiling water was placed on the hard, red-clay ground at the edge of the tarima just under one end of the palm roof.

Old Sharani was helped into a sitting position and her legs hung over the edge of the platform. In this way the steam would rise up into her cushma, something that had to occur simultaneously with the application of the tobacco paste. The stones heated by the fire were then put slowly into the water, one at a time, to create more heat, more steam.

During this procedure, the Brujo blew tobacco smoke constantly in the face of Aunt Sharani.

It is believed that if there has been any demon involved, the Brujo will be able to extract from the patient some small object, usually a little piece of bone or wood or straw, perhaps even a little pebble. This will then be declared the cause of the sickness. It will then be the Brujo's task to identify the demon who left this object on the victim.

The proceedings seemed to be taking forever. The Brujo seemed many miles away, lost in thought. Finally the water stopped steaming and Aunt Sharani was allowed to lie down once again. Every now and then in the silence a sigh could be heard from one of the onlookers or a dull moan from Sharani herself. All around the clearing were the little fireflies. They, too, are believed to be demons — demons with one bright eye, the "eye of death."

It was beginning to rain. Just a few drops. Big, heavy, deliberate drops. Everything seemed so awful. Would Aunt Sharani live?

The witch doctor now began his search. Very deliberately he began to scour the old woman's body. Under the drab, faded cushma his hand moved around slowly with the hope of identifying the source of the problem. Up, down, around. Back and forth. There was a brief hesitation before his hand reappeared from within the cushma and he held his palm open beneath the little candle for all to see.

Everyone crowded in. Sure enough, there it was. No bigger than a very small pea. A little particle of stone: coarse, rough, jagged, just the kind you see in the thousands each time you walk down the path to the stream for water. But it takes a Brujo to find it on a sick person. And only he can identify the culprit.

The silence was complete. No one moved. It was as though the very universe had become completely paralyzed. Everyone shared but one thought: Who was it? Who would be blamed? Who had done this to dear old Aunt Sharani?

And then of course the question: Would Aunt Sharani live? After a silence that seemed interminable, the Brujo, for the first time, spoke. "Who are the children here under the age of seven?" he intoned in a very low and stern voice.

Everyone looked toward Grandfather.

"Three boys and two girls," was Grandfather's laconic answer.

"Bring the two girls to me."

Grandfather looked toward Teni and Kiachi, the fathers of the two girls. Without a sign of protest, without so much as a murmur, the two men disappeared into the dark. They were strong and brave. Both were accomplished hunters. Both dreamed of someday taking their place as head man at the village campfire. It was not for them to show so much as one flicker of weakness.

For the women, it was different. When the two mothers broke out in loud crying and wailing, somehow they were expressing the sentiments of everyone present — including Teni and Kiachi, of course, for these two young men loved their little ones dearly.

Brujo spoke not a word, as though he was not even there.

Sleepy little Api and her friend Tania were carried in and given to their grieving mothers. Somehow everyone now seemed to cluster, perhaps in an unspoken sign of understanding and sympathy. Poor old Uncle sat mournfully holding the hand of his sick wife, glancing every now and then toward the two young mothers, feeling to blame for what was about to happen.

It did not take long for the witch doctor to make his pronouncement. He stared intently at the two girls, in spite of the mothers' attempts to hide their little ones from his penetrating gaze.

"It is she," he pronounced deliberately, pointing his finger straight at little Api, who was fast asleep. "She buried that stone along with sticks and splinters of bone under Sharani's hut. The cricket taught her."

"Oh, Teni," Keesha sobbed, "my little girl, my little girl. I cannot allow anything to happen to her. I hate the Brujo. I hate Aunt Sharani, I hate Grandfather. I hate life. All I want is Api. I want you, too, but most of all I want Api."

"But Keesha, my dear Keesha," Teni whispered to his wife, "Aunt Sharani has not died. Not yet. She may recover. In which case our little Api will be safe."

All they could do now was wait to see whether Sharani — and their Api — would survive.

Finally there was a commotion at the other end of the hut. Teni walked over to investigate.

He looked back at Keesha and said quietly, "Aunt Sharani has died."

Just then there was a brilliant flash of lightning. The sky lit up. Then the crash of thunder.

The witch doctor disappeared into the rainy night. He had done his job. Now the village must take over. Grandfather was in charge.

Keesha and Teni desperately wished that Api would be spared punishment, but they knew better. There is but one law in the jungle, and that law would be kept. The entire community would now have to take revenge on the spirit that had done so foul a deed.

Grandfather ordered everyone to their huts until dawn. In the morning they would meet on his tarima.

During that night, that sleepless night, Keesha thought of many things, including an escape into the forest with her little girl. She would not even have to tell Teni. But that would be worse. Who knows what spirits would await both of them there?

What followed the next morning was brief and according to the way of the Ashaninkas. In Grandfather's hut, Keesha was given the right to decide her daughter's fate. She could choose one of four deaths for her little girl: to be thrown off the cliff at Boca Tigre, to have her head clubbed, to be whipped to death with a lash made of the thorny and poisonous *shalanko*, or to be given to a Viracocha.

As Grandfather finished his list, which is the same made on all such occasions, Keesha crumpled to the tarima in a faint. Teni would have to make the decision. Grandfather turned toward him without a word.

Teni felt that he was also going to collapse, but he braced himself. The thought of Boca Tigre, with its whirlpool and its dreaded, bat-infested cliff, sent shivers down his spine. To witness Api's head clubbed would be more than he could bear. He might opt for her to be taken by the dreaded Viracocha, but none had been seen in the vicinity in ever so long.

"Shalanko, Grandfather," he said and, despite his attempt at bravery, broke into sobbing.

Within a matter of moments, the shalanko whips were prepared. Little Api, who had been playing beside her own tarima in spite of her mother's crying, was quietly tied to the nearest tree on the edge of the clearing. A whip was handed to each of the two men selected by Grandfather. Little Api stood there naked and wiggling, trying to get loose and crying for her mother, who by now had come around from her faint.

Api and Keesha's pleas were of no avail. The two older men readied themselves to get it over with. They secretly hated Grandfather for having chosen them.

In the brief silence of the men's hesitation, Teni shrieked, "Viracocha, Viracocha!" Everyone in the clearing looked toward the path that leads up from the stream. Sure enough, there stood a man and his wife. Two Viracocha. It was true that they did not wear cushmas and their hair was very short as through bats had chewed on it. Yet somehow they looked quite harmless.

"Grandfather! Grandfather!" shouted Teni, beside himself with confusion. "Please Grandfather, Keesha must decide. Keesha must decide."

Then he said to Keesha, "Please tell Grandfather that you choose for Api to be taken away by the Viracocha."

All but Teni and Grandfather drew back in fear as the white man came close. "What are you doing?" asked the male Viracocha in a low voice, speaking Ashaninka with an accent but quite clearly. "What is this you are preparing to do?"

Grandfather explained to the incredulous couple.

"Could we not take the little girl to live with us in La Merced?" asked the female Viracocha. "She could live with us. You would never see her again. Her spirit could not harm you, and we don't mind. Please, could we have her? You don't really want to kill her, do you?"

Grandfather looked toward Keesha. She must give the answer.

What would this frightened jungle woman decide? Her love for little Api was great. She could not bear to see her whipped to death. But would she allow for her to be taken away by these beings who came with deceitful words from the lake of the great serpent Nonki, where souls are collected in the stomach of a demon?

Keesha stood in silence, trembling. Teni held his breath. Then she spoke. She had made her decision. She looked Grandfather straight in the eye. "Grandfather," she said, "I give Api to Viracocha."

Keesha never saw her baby again.

⁓

This incident took place in the hilly jungle just behind Kimo. The white man's wife was Frida, Manuel Huaman's older sister. Manuel Huaman was our manager of the Kimo property.

I heard the story from Manuel himself and was anxious to meet Api. This I did some time later right at Kimo. She was stirring a big pot of bean soup over the open wood fire. She had come over the school vacation to help in the kitchen.

Unusually shy and quiet, this young Ashaninka girl would never venture into the Big Hut with the other kids, nor was it likely that her new mother, Frida, would ever take her to church. She must hear the gospel right there in the kitchen. The cooks and others coming in and out were Christians and the words of the music Api would hear were of Jesus.

"God," I prayed quietly, "this dear girl, spared from a most terrifying death — you must have had a reason. Surely it was to give her eternal life instead, as with many others, right here in Kimo."

Over the ensuing years she came often, always to the same smoky kitchen. She showed every sign of listening, but rarely spoke. She seemed deeply intent on a world all her own, as is the case with many who come to this remote place. But the seed was planted.

Sadly, at far too young an age, she became pregnant. Api died along with her baby in childbirth. I wish her story could have ended differently. But then, there is the reassuring promise of the faithful one: "My word will not return unto me void" (Isaiah 55:11) and the words of Jesus: "It is my Father's will that none should perish" (2 Peter 3:9).

I hope to see Api again some day and hear her finished story, this time not in a smoky kitchen, but in the presence of Jesus, who once said, "Suffer the little ones to come unto me, and forbid them not, for of such is the Kingdom of Heaven" (Mark 10:14).

13

SISKO
The Boy with Three Daddies

*Y*ou're about to read the story of Sisko, who lost his best friend — his father — and the rest of his family in a bloody massacre at the hands of the Shining Path in 1991. As terrible as this tragedy was, Sisko ended up gaining so much that he would become known as "the boy with three daddies."

In order to fully understand the story of Sisko's life, we must remember the path that led Isaac Salcedo to San Blas, where Sisko was orphaned.

Isaac, a converted street boy, is on Scripture Union's staff as Director of Bible Ministry in the Central Andes. He, too, has had more than one narrow escape.

On a particularly dull and cloudy day, three years before the massacre of Sisko's village, Isaac was hiking homeward on a remote path through the Andes. It was nearly a full day's walk up the mountain path from the big dusty road that joined two important towns. With the increased activity of Shining Path in the region, this road was constantly patrolled by regular troops. The troops were becoming increasingly tense. Their own behavior was often quite out of order. No Peruvian soldier or policeman wanted to be sent into the *zona roja* (red zone), even if it did mean an increase in an otherwise very low salary. They were often sitting ducks for the terrorists, usually outwitted and often outnumbered by them.

Isaac was a man of God. His mission was different. It was to bring Christ's love and peace to the community of Estancia at the top of the hill. He knew how to do this. It was not by bringing them news of troop activities on the main road or of the government boasting of victory. It was by sharing God's eternal message of hope that transcends all human effort. He encouraged the few Quechua Christians that night, sold a few Bibles in the village the next day, and then started down the path.

He was hot and thirsty when he reached the bottom, but it was well worth it for the number of Bibles he had sold in Estancia. In fact, he had sold them all. It certainly made walking easier.

He stepped out onto the road just as a small army patrol passed by. One of the soldiers grabbed him by the arm. Isaac instinctively tried to pull away. "No, no," said the soldier, tightening his grip. "You stay right close to me."

"Why are you taking me?" protested Isaac.

"You'll find out when we get to the garrison."

"But I ..."

"You had better keep quiet, keep walking, and try not to cause yourself a bigger problem."

Isaac knew. He could put two and two together. "Father," he prayed quietly, "if it be your will, spare me once again."

They proceeded around three bends and down a long stretch of road to the army post. Rustic, almost primitive, it had obviously been patched together hurriedly. The army did not have much money. Supplies were short and the men were overworked. All they wanted was to get all this behind them and go straight home. They were more interested in winning the war against terrorism than in bringing about justice. Whatever the cost, even the loss of innocent lives, it was worth it. The ends justified the means, and after all, "Everyone makes mistakes." Everything was pointing to Isaac as another of the mistakes.

"I caught this man," said the soldier, shoving him in front of an officer in charge. "Picked him right off the path to Estancia. A Senderista if I ever saw one."

"What do you have to say for yourself?" asked the young officer along with an assortment of oaths.

"I went up to Estancia to sell Bibles. I am an *evangélico*."

That did it.

"You look like an evangelical Bible seller," scorned the officer. "You also look like a Senderista just back from telling those ignorant mountain people about your Chairman Gonzalo and all the good he will do when he overthrows the government and has soldiers like me hanging from every light post in Lima."

"Please, please," implored Isaac, "send someone, anyone, up to Estancia to check on my story. God be my judge. I am not lying."

"The Peruvian Army doesn't need your help, sir, to arrive at conclusions and reach its verdict," said the officer sarcastically.

He snapped his fingers. Two young soldiers stepped up. "Take this man to the *paredón* (wall). Shoot him."

They picked up a weapon and led Isaac out, up the same long stretch and around the first bend. Isaac's heart and mind struggled furiously within him for his attention. In a few short minutes, what should he think, what should he pray? If given a chance, what should he say?

"Oh God, have mercy on me. Please take care of Clementina and the boys. Lord, they'll grow up without a father. Please, Jesus, please ..."

His anguish of soul was stopped short when he saw another officer approaching. As he drew closer, Isaac noted that he was of higher rank. Isaac pulled toward the left, bringing his soldier escort with him. He was now in front of the officer. With his arms still firmly in the grip of the two young men, he fell to his knees and pleaded, "Sir, you are a high-ranking officer. You can save me if you will. Please, I beg you. Look into my eyes and tell me: Are they the eyes of a Shining Path terrorist or are they the eyes of a man who so loves God that he walks days on end to places like Estancia to sell Bibles and teach people about Jesus?"

The officer looked straight into Isaac's eyes. Then, turning to the soldiers, he commanded crisply, "Let this man go."

~

San Blas was just one more of the tiny villages along the mule trail that took the occasional traveler down from the very highest mountain pass into the deep valley seven thousand feet below. From above, it looked quaint: a collection of small, red-tiled roofs supported by thick adobe mud walls. The two pine trees stood out. Someone must have gone to great pains to make them grow, because San Blas was just above the timber line. From below, the village was nothing short of impressive. Jutting out from the cliff, it looked as though it had been built on a saucer left carelessly at the edge of a table.

Everyone knew each other in San Blas. They all considered themselves Blasenos and were proud to live in the province of Junin where the great Simón Bolívar had defeated the Spaniards. Everyone spoke Quechua, the language of their Inca ancestors, and the more enterprising, like Venancio, spoke Spanish, too.

"Papá, Papá, agarra ésta, si puedes" (Daddy, Daddy, catch this one if you can). Eight-year-old Sisko ran toward the well-worn soccer ball and kicked it right past his father, his best friend. They both ran down the slope after the ball, hand in hand.

"Let's do it again, Papá. You're the best player in San Blas."

That was the biggest compliment Venancio could receive from his little boy, but he had more important things to see to that afternoon. "I must go now, Sisko," he said. "You go with your friends to play in the Plaza." He tried a smile and waved goodbye.

Sisko had recently seen this sad look on his Daddy's face quite often. But if something was wrong, there was no need to worry. Daddy would fix it. After all, there was only one Daddy like his.

Meanwhile, at home, Sisko's mother, Lucrecia, left baby Tino with Dorita as she went out in search of her other six. She knew where to find them. They would be playing tag in the Plaza. It had been raining, so the unpaved streets were uneven and muddy.

"Vamos chicos" (Let's go, kids), she called out hesitatingly. She knew they were having fun. It somehow didn't seem that long ago since she herself played tag there. Sisko raced past her, a neighbor in hot pursuit.

"Ya, Sisko, vamos!"

Sisko was now "it," so he could slow down.

"But Mama, the sun hasn't gone down yet. There's an inch of it still left," he begged.

Mama smothered a smile. "No, Sisko, the sun was behind the hill before I came out for you."

Mothers shouldn't have favorites, and Lucrecia claimed not to, but she adored Sisko, especially his big smile. She had first seen it in his dimpled cheek the day he was born.

They had *cuy* (guinea pig) for supper that night. Always a treat.

"Me gusta" (I like it), said four-year-old Javier. He was their fat little boy.

"Glad he's still little," chimed in Manuel, "or he'd eat it all."

"Right," said Dorita. "He probably would eat our whole pig by himself."

They all laughed, even Javier, too young to know what was going on. The pig they all knew about. He was being fattened up for Christmas, but that was a long time off yet.

Dawn the following morning was bright and sunny. It was still early and the kids had not yet gone to school. Sisko was in the patio. A patio in an Andean dwelling is a square courtyard surrounded by the rooms of the house. Everything opens into the patio. In the case of Venancio, that also included the *granja*, where the animals lived. Because every house is built up against the next one, there is usually room for only a door and a couple of small windows onto the street. All whitewashed and under a handmade tile roof, it made a beautiful home for Sisko.

In fact, he was playing marbles with his brother on the baked clay patio floor when his world fell apart. He heard a crash and the sound of splintering. It was the front door.

"¡Venancio traidor!" shouted a man, almost incoherent with rage.

"Venancio ... why, that's Papá," thought Sisko. "He's no traitor." But that was just the tip of the iceberg. What followed was so con-fusing, so utterly chaotic.

"Venancio, Venancio," he kept hearing. "Su mujer también" (His woman also).

"Sácala, sácala" (Get her out, get her out), Sisko heard them yell and then saw his mother being thrown down on the patio floor.

As children screamed and the terrorists madly searched every room, Sisko took refuge in the granja with the pig.

"Acá está" (Here he is), whooped one of the men, followed by cheers from the rest. Seconds later, Venancio, bleeding, was brought out into the patio and slammed down beside his wife, who by now mercifully appeared to be unconscious. What happened next defies description. In respect for Sisko, I will not give the details. Suffice it to say that before he fainted, he witnessed more than a child ever should. His mother and sisters were raped. Then they, along with his father and brothers, including little Javier and baby Tino, were stoned to death.

When Sisko came to, he was hidden behind the pig. Aside from the usual clucking of the hens and the scurrying around of guinea pigs, the world was silent. One look into the patio and Sisko was gone again. Small wonder. Later he stumbled out the front door and read a sign written in his family's blood: "Death to whoever touches these bodies. Traitors must all die like dogs."

Eighteen children were left that day with one thing in common: they had all seen their parents killed. Some of them were brothers and sisters. Others, like Sisko, were now entirely alone.

He spent the next few days wandering aimlessly through the town. Because all of his family, including him, were supposed to have died, no one wanted to be seen taking the sole survivor in. Who was to know the identity of the informers left behind? There was no trust left in San Blas, only fear and subdued rage. Sisko had to sleep outside and eat food that the frightened villagers left hidden for the last of Venancio's family. The house had by now been burned and the bodies left to decompose.

When Scripture Union learned about the massacre, Isaac was sent to set up a camp for the young victims. He was given the details of the massacre. The eighteen orphans would be in the camp. They had all been taken in by a brave Christian man and his wife, who eagerly awaited Isaac's visit.

"I'm going to San Blas," announced Isaac one evening. Clementina was used to this.

"How long will you be?"

"Who knows? Depends what I find."

"A week?" asked Clementina.

"Yes, a week," laughed Isaac, "or maybe two." He threw his arms around his wife. They had lived this way for years. Serving God together. Rearing their four boys. Never knowing what the next day would bring, yet somehow enjoying it all. "God's business, you know," he often told me.

Scripture Union, on more than one occasion, had offered to evacuate Isaac and family to a safer place than the Central Andes region, which was particularly treacherous due to the intensity of terrorist activity. Clementina had stuck firmly to her husband. "This is the place to which God has called us," she said, with a smile that reflected a peaceful heart.

"Just go, Isaac," Clementina said, "but don't ask me to go with you. It was bad enough when we walked." She was alluding to the motorcycle Christian friends had recently given him for his travels.

By noon of the following day, Isaac had left the vehicle with a friend at the top of the range and was well on his way toward San Blas. He went over in his mind the plans he had for the Scripture

Union camp he hoped to set up for the children of the three villages on the ledge overhanging the jungle.

When he got to San Blas, the scene was as horrific as he expected, but he found that suitable preparations had been made. Sufficient corn, potatoes, and haba beans for the children had been assembled. As for the program, it would definitely not be carried out in the best Scripture Union tradition, but would nevertheless accomplish the purpose of giving the children a restorative week and a personal encounter with God.

It was a good camp, though on the somber side, as would be expected. Eternity seemed closer to those kids than the soccer field, and the possibility of really talking to God was more exciting than the normal chit-chat on rainy days. During that camp, God allowed a deep relationship to develop between Isaac and the children. As the camp ended, the eighteen frightened kids asked Isaac to be their daddy.

This was the beginning of Kawayhusasi (home to live in), the home Scripture Union set up right in San Blas. It was three weeks before Isaac got back to Clementina. She wept when she heard why he had taken so long. She was particularly pleased to hear that her brave husband had adopted eighteen lonely orphans.

Over the course of the next few months, Sisko gave what was left of his shattered life to Jesus. Our Lord filled the big, empty space that had been left deep inside. He slowly changed fear into trust, bad dreams into quiet sleep. Sisko's big smile returned. He began his prayers with the words, "Dear Daddy ..."

Sisko flourished in the care of Isaac and the others. He finished primary school seven years later, at the age of fifteen. Not long after that, Isaac was glad to see a Christian friend of his offer Sisko a piece of land where he could plant yuca and bananas. Sisko could go fishing with them, and the man would keep an eye on the boy.

———

Some years later, Isaac visited again and found Sisko happily married and with his own little baby, Tino. He is satisfied living on what they have, unconcerned about what they may not have tomorrow.

Seated on Sisko's tarima bark floor under the simplest thatched roof, Isaac surveyed the little family with deep gratitude.

Lightning gashed the black sky. Thunder rocked the mighty forest.

Isaac looked at the little family, tears of joy in his eyes. "Sisko," he thought, "my dear son, Sisko. Hot, oh so hot, was the fire in which you were forged." Then out loud he said, "Someday, Sisko, you will come forth as gold, for he who has begun a good work in you will perform it until the day of Jesus Christ."

"Yes," said Sisko as he looked through the storm. "On that day, I'll be with my three daddies — forever."

14

AROLDO
Butterfly on a Rainy Day

The boy called him "father" and the father called him "son." He called his brother "brother" and his mother "mother." These were the headwater Machiguenga, south of Kimo, for whom there is no time, no property, no need of names. The next family lives six hours downriver. The nine thousand in the tribe live widely scattered over a very large expanse of unspoiled virgin forest, lush and beautiful.

It's a simple life. What more do you need in order to plant yuca and banana, fish, hunt with bow and arrow, and build huts and everything else, with poles, palm leaves, and the bejuco vine?

This might seem like paradise, but it most definitely is not. How can you enjoy a flock of brilliant macaws or little green parrots when their voices are the disembodied voices of the dead? How can you sit on a warm rock down beside the sparkling stream and enjoy the cool, fresh breeze when that, too, comes from the Underworld? Above all, how could you ever break free when only too soon the sun will set and the jungle will burst into darkness and demon life?

"Tell me the story again, Father," he begged, "I won't sleep till you finish. I promise."

The man adjusted his cotton cushma gown and poked at the fire. "Don't you want the one about the white-breasted swallow?"

"No, I want the one about the moon," he insisted.

"Very well. In the beginning men collected dust and cooked it and ate it. They called it yuca."

The eight-year-old laughed as he always did at this part of the story.

"But the first daughter refused to eat it. She ate real yuca which the Moon had brought her. Just after midnight of the last day of her enclosure period, like all Machiguenga girls, she was brought out, scalded, made to vomit, and given a haircut. By dawn she was ready to enter her new hut. When she went in, she found the Moon there. He had come to ask for her hand.

"All was well until the daughter had a baby. This made the mother angry. Her daughter was still too young. She hemorrhaged and died. The Moon blamed his mother-in-law and she blamed him. He took the body on to a beach farther downriver and left it there while he took his boy into the sky. The mother-in-law discovered this and became very angry now, because the worst thing for them was to have their bodies left unburied, food for birds and animals. She insulted the Moon. Losing his patience, he turned her into a wild pig, killed and chopped her up, and took her to the sky.

"His older boy he made into the Sun. Sometimes he gets angry and scorches the Earth in order to dry up the yuca. The New Moon sits in the sky, eating meat from his backpack. He eats very slowly, killing one pregnant woman after another as he slowly fills his belly.

"So," he said, finishing up his story, "remember, my boy, to take careful watch over the yuca. Never let it go to waste. Never anger the Moon. We want to stay in our bodies. We don't want to die."

"Thank you, Father," said the boy, "I want to grow to be big and strong like you. I will live long like Grandfather. Someday around my fire I will tell my son the stories, especially this one about the Moon. I'll tell them never to anger him, because we don't want to die."

"You must have had a terrible fright," one of the Machigengua said to Harold Davis during his first visit to Peru in 1959. "You are so white."

"No, no," said Harold. "Wait till you meet my wife and children! We are all white. That is the way Kirinko are born, but we are really just like you."

Harold knew what he was thinking. Just like us? Pink skin, blue eyes, hair on their faces, the strangest things on their feet? Arriving in a gigantic wooden bee, unable to talk properly?

But over the coming years, Harold and Pat Davis and their kids, Neil and Rosemary, learned to love the people of this remote tribe. For many years in the jungle, they would throw their lot in with theirs, for better or for worse — all for the sake of the one who had said, "Go into all the world and preach the gospel" (Mark 16:15).

Harold had had a rather unhappy childhood, which gave him a natural ability to empathize. A shy man, somewhat of a loner, he developed a profound love for the Machigengua, especially their children. Aroldo, as they called him, would often be seen going down the trail, whistling, with three or four kids vying with one another to take hold of his hands. He laughed with them, cried with them, and would regularly sit with them on their tarima floor, just passing the time away.

One of them was the boy who had sat beside his father years before, listening to the story about the Moon. He was now sixteen. He had been given the name Gregorio and was one of Aroldo's favorites. He had an incredible love of life and shared his enthusiasm for birds, for jungle sounds, for the unexpected surprise at a bend in the meandering river. The phrase "still waters run deep" was surely true in the case of Aroldo and his young friend. Life in the jungle may sound boring to an outsider, but it certainly wasn't for these two. With similar agendas for the future, each in his own way quietly looked forward to a long life of adventure and fulfillment.

But like a tropical rainstorm arriving with no warning, disaster struck. A plague of measles hit the Machigengua. Harold and Pat witnessed the horrors of the full-blown disease: severe vomiting; diarrhea; painful irritation of the nostrils, mouth, and lips; itchy skin; wrenching cough; soaring fever; and finally pneumonia.

Aroldo carried a gravely ill Gregorio to his own bedroom and never moved from his side, giving him medication and liquids every ten minutes, day and night.

Gregorio lapsed into semi-consciousness and began to thrash in what Aroldo learned later was the onset of encephalitis. As the boy struggled, he screamed in terror, "I'm dying! I'm dying!" Although they had medications, there were no tranquilizers to calm the agony.

As far as was known, Gregorio had never accepted Christ as Savior. The deeply ingrained terror all Machiguengas have of death and their future in the spirit world was upon him. As Gregorio thrashed and screamed, Aroldo spoke into his ears some of the few words of Machiguenga he knew: "God so loved the world — you Gregorio — that he sent his only son Jesus, so that if you believe, Gregorio, you will not die but have life forever."

"No, but I'm dying! I'm dying!" he cried.

"God so loved the world ..."

"I'm dying!"

Over and over, for what seemed an eternity, into an ear that no longer seemed able to listen, Aroldo repeated the message. Finally Gregorio became too weak to scream, but he continued to thrash until finally he died.

Aroldo hoped with all his heart that Gregorio would live forever with his Savior. The boy's death had not been easy for him to accept.

Years passed, but the memory of Gregorio left an indelible mark on Aroldo. And the Davis family's encounters with death were far from over.

⸺

The lights twinkled and most of the presents were now wrapped and under the tree. There was excitement in the air. It was December 24, 1971, and the little house smelled of Christmas cookies and other goodies that Pat was quickly finishing up as the kids darted in and out of the kitchen door. When not at home in the tribe with the Machiguengas, they were here in Yarina, jungle base of the Wycliffe Bible Translators. Both places were home, and for the kids both were fun to be in, but Yarina was definitely the better place to be on Christmas Eve.

They had come on ahead and their daddy was to join them soon. He was returning from Machiguenga Land, as he called it, by way of Cuzco and Lima, and his flight was due in any time now. The van would pick him and the other four missionaries up and bring them on home. So there was no time to be wasted. The kids couldn't wait till midnight, and Mom was trying to slow the clock down as she finally got the last batch of cookies out of the oven.

"Good," she said, throwing off her apron. "That's that. Now let's sit down and I'll read you a Christmas story."

On the far side of the Andes, Harold Davis stood up and was one of the first in line when LANSA Airlines announced that flight 361 was boarding for Pucallpa. He was pleased with himself because he had just managed to catch the flight, having spent the last two hours scurrying around Lima in search of a loaf of pan baguette, which he and Pat so enjoyed every time they were out in the big city.

The sky over Kimo was beautiful. It was one of those dark, moonless nights when the stars seem so bright and close that you feel you could stretch up and pick one off the top of a tree. As was the case every Monday, Wednesday, and Friday, there was one little "star" that moved across the sky ever so slowly. With a bit of imagination, you could even hear it before it disappeared in the east.

On this Christmas Eve, though, as the "star" crossed the sky, there was an explosion that no one heard, a flash that no one saw. Then silence. It was all over. Aroldo was gone.

Christmas was not Christmas that following day for Pat and Neil and Rosemary. In fact, it has never been the same since. There will forever be a missing chair in the mind, if not at the table, an empty spot in the heart, if not under the tree. The memory of the long vigil that night at the airport where Aroldo was supposed to arrive may no longer haunt, but it will forever remain. The thought of Daddy's first Christmas in heaven would take on a new and beautiful meaning, but would always somehow hurt.

Each had to process the events of that day and of the following ten days in their own way before the bodies were found in the jungle, yet all three would come out on the victory side.

Victory for Pat meant going back to Machiguenga Land, this time alone. True, with her little ones, but still alone. Could she face life in the land of the Red Indian without Aroldo? Could she bear to hear the strange jungle sounds in the night and reach out and touch the empty hammock beside hers? Now she would have to make all the decisions — for herself, for her children, for the future — alone. Many were praying, but it was still rough, and she knew that the path ahead would be anything but rosy. Raw fear often gripped her soul.

She could understand in a new way what it must be like to be a Machiguenga. Then she remembered the lines from Arnie Flint's famous poem: "God hath not promised skies always blue, / Flower-strewn pathways all our lives through; / But God hath promised ..." Pat Davis would become living proof of the bounty and goodness and presence of God in the face of death.

In the forest, everyone knows that the part of the tree that lives comes from the part that dies. Although at that moment she was not aware of it, Pat was now perfectly positioned to demonstrate the incarnation: to put flesh on the great truths of God that she and Harold had worked so hard to make alive to their Indian friends. When she was tempted to think of Harold as a butterfly on a rainy day when its wings are stuck together and it cannot fly, she also had to remember that a butterfly lives but one day, yet has time enough.

Just as a neighboring tribe didn't believe the missionaries to be truly human until little David Weber skinned his knee and they saw it bleed, so the Indians in Pat's clearing believed in her in a new and very different way once they saw her suffer. The price may have been a very big one to pay, but Harold's death had not been in vain.

The big wood bee flew in and the villagers ran out to meet it.

"Where is Aroldo?" they shouted, as Pat stepped out of the little Cessna. Harold always got off first to help her down. "Where is he, where is he?" The women held back, but the little kids ran around, "Aroldo, Aroldo," and the men pressed their noses against the window of the now empty plane, surprised.

Pat took a deep breath. "He died," she said bluntly. There were tears in her eyes, and they saw them. "He was in a big wood bee," she continued, "and it fell right out of the sky into the jungle."

"What happened to his body?" was the obvious question every Indian asked at this point.

"No one found it until after ten days," she answered softly. She knew what they were thinking: about the birds, about the animals, about the horror of remaining unburied. Pat herself had thought about all that, but knew that Harold was safe "with Christ, which is far better" (Philippians 1:21). She longed to tell them, to have them truly understand.

"We thought Kirinko never died," said one of the men, as he helped little Rosemary up onto the tarima floor of their jungle house.

"Our little children get the fever and die," piped in one of the women. "Yours always go away and the Wood Bee brings them back well. Now you are crying."

After a fairly long silence, Pat spoke up, choosing her words carefully. "Nokenkisukeaka kantankicha tera nontsaroge" (I am sad but not afraid), she said.

They sat around just looking at her. They watched every move, analyzed her slightest gesture. None of her sadness or suffering was lost to them. They had heard her. Now they saw and perceived it all. They looked at each other, then back at her. Not a word was spoken. No sound was made.

Not as a bolt of lightning that suddenly dazzles the evening sky, but more like a morning mist that rises and is slowly replaced by the brightness of day, they finally understood. Aroldo had been real. What he and Pat had told them many times was true.

Only now did God speak Machiguenga.

15

MANOLO
A Street Boy of Valor

*B*ig, strong, handsome, and brave, Manolo is a hero today to every boy in Girasoles and Kimo. As Manolo has grown step by step as a Christian, many of us have matured alongside him.

A lookout, precariously perched on a ledge above Kimo, was a perfect place for me to begin to talk to Manolo back in 1998. The sights, the sounds, and the smells all brought back memories for Manolo: memories that perhaps he had tried to forget, yet many of which still needed healing.

What we often call Mi Verdad (My Truth) is that carefully guarded space inside where you keep both the memories you cherish and the memories that haunt you. For every street boy, Mi Verdad stores a dark side, the door to which is only opened by permission.

In those days when Manolo had first come to Kimo, in the noiseless rush of a mind racing past reason, he cursed the city and toyed with the haunting memory of a rain-wet jungle. There were parts of his past that he could not forget. Desperately, he tried to put his thinking into order, but glue and repeated beatings had taken their toll. On that jungle lookout, Manolo struggled to tell me his story.

He had lived his first twelve years in Iquitos. His mother's last words to him, as he left his home never to return, were, "Hijo, nunca llores por mi" (Son, don't ever cry for me). These were the words that would resound and echo back and forth in his tormented mind for many years to come.

"Don't ever cry for me," he repeated. "And I never did. I often wished I could, though. I always loved my mother. I still do. I would give anything to hear her voice, just once again. I wonder if she ever thinks of me."

He was one of eleven children. His father was in prison and Manolo loved him very much. He always went with his mother to visit. He remembers walking along beside her carrying some food and handing it himself to his dad. "I always felt so sad when we came out from the big gates, leaving him behind."

When Manolo's father was eventually released, he slowly killed himself with drugs and alcohol.

"I remember him crying aloud and screaming in pain, day after day," Manolo told me. "The very worst day in my life was when I came into the house and found him dead."

That was when Manolo was nine. From then on, his mother had the impossible task of keeping all her children alive. Manolo's job was to go to Puerto Belén early each morning to steal food for the rest of them to eat. With his father gone, he took to drugs. For the next three years he stole not only for food but to buy glue and the deadly coca paste. Things for the young Manolo just kept getting worse and worse.

"From the day I threw a brick at my mother, I knew I had to go," Manolo continued, tossing a little pebble down into the stream below. The last flames of love and care had finally sputtered and disappeared, leaving hot embers that glowed and dropped cold ashes. Manolo felt dirty, nasty, unclean. From then on, every insult hurled his way seemed less to him than he deserved.

He went down to the Varadero where the boats are loaded, the same place where we had said goodbye to Luis Luna. He slipped aboard unnoticed and hid behind the sacks of cargo next to the propeller shaft. It was dark, hot, and steamy, and during the six-day voyage upriver to Pucallpa, he ate nothing and drank only the water that seeped into the bottom of the boat. He slipped down the landing ramp as if helping to carry off lighter cargo.

Countless children twelve years of age and much younger work in the streets of this town, but they have someone who gives them a job. For a street boy there is no one. So many people had disappointed him in the past that he learned to put his faith in the only one who would not let him down: himself.

In Lima, his life became a kaleidoscope of twisting and turning experiences of all sizes and shapes and colors, mostly dark. The river was now far behind him, and so was his long freezing journey across the Andes, stowed away in the back of a truck. He remembers when he ate garbage shared with stray dogs on Jirón de La Unión in Lima and shivered in the dark on damp, cold nights in which many others died of pneumonia. He knew that his body, too, would some day be picked up and thrown into La Fosa Común (the common pit).

"My happiest day was when I met other abandoned boys in Plaza San Martín in Lima," Manolo said. "My greatest fear is loneliness. The sound of my own voice in the breeze is hollow."

He had terrifying encounters with the police. "They accused me of stealing a woman's purse," he said. "I hadn't, but they said I had and that I was to put my fingerprint on a paper saying I had. I refused. They said they would throw me in the dungeon. I felt hot inside. I was angry, but I had learned that it is better not to say anything. In the dungeon, another man came in and said the same thing. I held my ground. He then said that if I didn't confess, I would be taken to the chamber. You know, the place where they torture. I was so hot inside that I didn't care, so they took me. Fortunately, they didn't get their electric wires out, like they did to César. Remember?"

"Yes, I do," I answered.

"Or set their police dogs on me. They hit me on the head, over and over. Still I would say nothing. Then they started punching my face. They had blood all over their hands. They punched and punched until I could hardly see. But I never said a word. It made them angry and they kept punching. Finally I fell down. My face was like a piece of meat. Then they stopped and went out. Another man came in and kicked me back into the street. I hadn't stolen the purse."

And there are other parts of this boy's life that it would not be proper for me to mention.

He strayed into Centro Girasoles one day, filthy, ragged, and angry. But here his life was to be changed around. The stories of Satan sounded so much more like his real world, but it was the ones about Jesus he most liked to hear.

One day, some months after his arrival, Manolo sat alone, tipping his chair forward and staring at the grease spots on the dining room floor. "Jesus, Jesus," he repeated to himself. His power to raise the dead, heal the sick, still the storm: all this was new to him. Never before had he heard of such a person. He sat up suddenly. Could all this be true? This incredible person who had risked touching a leper … maybe he would even have touched a street boy.

Manolo struggled to accept God's forgiveness and overcome the powerful self-hatred that had been a way of life all his long years as a child criminal who'd been sent away by his own mother. He wept and wept.

"Manolo," said Pablo, "God has forgiven you." He placed his hand gently on the broad shoulders of this dear boy. "You must believe me this time."

Manolo looked up and straight into the eyes of the man who had become like a father to him. "Oh, but you don't know who you are looking at," he said.

Actually, Pablo pretty much did. But he knew God also. "Remember, Manolo?" he asked, once again quoting Isaiah 1:18: "Though your sins be like scarlet, they shall be as white as snow; though they be as red as crimson, they shall be like wool."

"Oh, but my sins, Hermano Pablo, my sins," he sobbed. "You don't know me, you don't know me."

"But that's not the point, Manolo," Pablo said. "I don't, but God does, and that is the point. He is the one who knows, and he is the one who has forgiven you. Remember how free you felt that day when you first asked his forgiveness and accepted his pardon? You're as free today as you were then. And what's more, he's forgotten your sin. It's Satan who hasn't, and he is the one causing you so much grief. So send him back to hell where he belongs."

⁓

Like so many of our boys, Manolo is probably not fully aware of how important he has become, not only to Nestor and Tino whom he defended in the restaurant, but to many others as well. Through Manolo's witnessing in the streets, God is bringing boys to himself. And through the miraculous choreography of Manolo's life, he is renewing the faith and commitment of many gringos.

One occasion a couple of years ago I remember very well. I was walking down our Lima office stairs to say goodbye to a medical team that had been serving in Peru for a few weeks. They had asked to meet our abandoned street boys before returning home. I noticed a bit of a stir below and hoped it wasn't one of our guests being ripped off by some passing thief. (Our corner had recently been distinguished by the city's leading newspaper as the most dangerous in Lima.)

Fortunately, it wasn't that. It was one of the doctors, a big, six-foot-five man who had suddenly burst into tears. He got himself under control and his group boarded taxis and were away. That evening our good friend, Opal Hardgrove, leader of many such teams, phoned to say that the doctor was OK. He had just been overcome by his emotions. He told her that he hadn't cried for years, but that he had been profoundly affected by what he had seen upstairs in our third-floor Girasoles auditorium.

There, with the rest of the team, he had witnessed the story of Juan, Andrés, and Manolo put to music and acted out by the three boys themselves.

The power of Almighty God to reach into those totally shattered young lives and to transform them into three beautiful radiant young men has brought tears to many an eye and renewed faith to many a fainting heart.

The story is told in three scenes with several secondary actors. The boys themselves choose who will interpret each part and insist that each be represented by a boy acting out his present role in life. They will allow only two, for example, to act the part of Jesus, and the roles of boys in the streets inhaling glue are given to those who are still doing that. So never is the play acted out twice the same.

In the first scene, Manolo comes out as a Lima street boy and sees Jesus hanging dead on a cross. He is confused, sad, then angry. "You told us that you would never die," he says. "We believed you. You were good to people like us in the street. Why did you lie to us? So you were just another big person mocking us!"

Manolo collapses to the ground dejected, disillusioned. The body is carried out. Then an earthquake awakens him. He looks up to see Jesus coming toward him. In a scene reminiscent of Michelangelo's *Creation*, in which the finger of God touches that of man, Manolo is transformed by the touch of the Living Christ.

In the second part, Manolo experiences the struggle of every new Christian between God's Spirit and the tempter's voice. For this boy on stage and in real life, it is a bitter struggle, a battle to the finish. Manolo puts every fiber of his body into the enactment. After all, he lives it every day with memories that torment, shallow scars that cover deep wounds, and a self-image struggling to be remade. When he says, "Es mi lucha de cada día" (It is my daily struggle), he speaks of experience born in hell and a life now destined for Heaven. Praise God.

"Hombres de Valor" (Men of Valor) is the final part. Here the three young men, emboldened by their commitment to the Savior, go out into the dark streets of Lima in search of other boys. So that those boys, too, will meet the one who walked the streets in loneliness, who was tortured and killed; the one who died but lives.

And so the cycle in Girasoles and Kimo will continue ... until he comes.

TELL US GOD HAS NOT FORGOT

From the street's end I am calling,
From the heat and dirt and rot,
Where the bleak and fearsome footsteps
Lead to us whom God forgot.
No one comes to our dark corner,
`Tis a long neglected spot.
No one hears our cry at midnight,
We are those whom God forgot.
We are lonely, hungry, hunted,
Life is short, death is our lot,
We've no history, we've no future,
Can it be that God forgot?
In the whisper of the breezes,
In the silent realms of thought,
There are stirrings, strange, insistent,
But what matters, God forgot.
At the alley's end we're waiting,
Blindly hope, we know not what.
Only do not let us perish
Thinking still that God forgot.
In the smog and stench of dying
From which children cannot run,
There are hearts and minds still open,

There is sowing to be done.
In the dens of sin and darkness,
There are battles to be fought.
At the street's end tell the story,
Tell us God has not forgot.

— PAUL CLARK